MY RIO DE JANEIRO

A COOKBOOK

MY RIO DE JANEIRO
A COOKBOOK

LETICIA MOREINOS SCHWARTZ

Food Photography by Kate Sears

K

Published in 2013 by Kyle Books
www.kylebooks.com
Distributed by National Book Network
4501 Forbes Blvd., Suite 200
Lanham, MD 20706
Phone: (800) 462-6420
Fax: (800) 338-4550
customercare@nbnbooks.com

10 9 8 7 6 5 4 3 2 1
ISBN: 978-1-909487-01-7

Project Editor Anja Schmidt
Designer Two Associates
Food Photographer Kate Sears
Food Styling Paul Grimes
Prop Styling PJ Mehaffey
Copy Editor Leda Scheintaub
Production Nic Jones and David Hearn

Library of Congress Control No. 2013912211

Color reproduction by ALTA London
Printed and bound in China

INTRODUCTION

I am horrible with dates, but one date I don't ever forget is February 17, 1997, the day I moved to New York to study culinary arts and devote my life to cooking. I am usually very emotional, and looking back at that date, I am surprised at my big smile while my family was bursting into tears at the airport farewell. In retrospect, I knew that day that this book was somewhere in my future—and the reason for my big smile.

It took me over a decade to turn my passion for cooking into a career. I went to cooking school, worked in restaurants, studied food journalism, and soon enough I was the proud author of *The Brazilian Kitchen*, my first cookbook.

After the book came out, I started my blog, chefleticia.com, which documents my discoveries around Brazil. With blogging, I integrated writing and photography into my cooking life. While I am not a professional photographer, I took many of the photos featured in this book.

Throughout my travels (though there is so much I still have to see!), I began to realize that my love for Brazil is as big as the country—but my heart belongs to Rio de Janeiro. I also realized that my life was shaped by the foods in Rio, and that much of what I do today is linked to something in Rio. From the juices I drink every morning, like Limonada Suíssa (page 34), and the sandwiches I eat for lunch, like Chicken Salad with Carrots and Chives on Whole Wheat (page 135), to the sweets I serve at my kids' birthday parties, like Brigadeiro (page 27)—it's all about Rio.

FINDING RIO'S CULINARY HEART

When I set out to write this book, I wanted to bring the cuisines of Rio to the same popular level as our other assets: the beach, music, samba, Carnival, and soccer. This meant getting to the heart of Rio's most talented people and discovering the most delicious recipes.

I met some incredible chefs like Kátia Barbosa from Aconchego Carioca, Portuguese cooks like Manuela Arraes, home cooks like Ivani de Souza Ferreira, and many more, all of whom you'll find here in this book. I was amazed by their knowledge, their simple approach to cooking, and the wonder of their recipes.

I am fascinated by Brazilian culture: we are a mixture of African, Portuguese and native Indian influences—and we are proud of our origins. This mixture can be seen in the music we hear, in the foods that we eat, and in the faces of our people. In different parts of the country, however, you will find one dominant influence over the others. And in Rio, my friend, it tastes like Portugal. The cooking of Rio is dominated by the lusitanic flavors of salt cod, onions, garlic, bay leaves, and egg yolk pastries—flavors that are bright and alive in the pages of this book.

I go back home at least twice a year with my kids, and we spend a good chunk of time in Rio (though never enough), especially during the summer. I explore my hometown with the eyes of a hungry carioca woman who misses home. I take my kids all over Rio, and we go on frequent trips to the outskirts of Rio, like Búzios, Paraty, Teresópolis and Petrópolis—neighborhoods included in this book. As I explored the city with a new perspective, I came to discover a Rio completely different from the one I left.

When I left for America, the food culture in Rio was nothing compared to the magnitude of today's trends. At that time, Confeitaria Colombo at Centro was one of the biggest bakeries in Rio. And their ham and cheese

BACALHAU
SEM PELE MACRO
R$ 55,00 KG

BACALHAU
LOMBO MORHUA 7/9
R$ 42,00 KG

folheado (page 120) remains my favorite! Today, however, you'll find modern bakeries specializing in different treats like cupcakes, macarons, and chocolates. The only English you'd hear in the 90s was from tourists, while today, there are people from all over the world living and working in Rio.

Brazil is changing, and Rio is changing with it. Over the past decade, my hometown has boomed, restoring itself to the global stage as a portal for two huge world events: The World Cup in Spring 2014 and the Olympics two years later.

Not coincidentally, dining in Rio gets better all the time. Many new restaurants are opening, and Rio is becoming quite a culinary contender. Rio doesn't aspire to be fancy, but we do aspire to eat delicious, amazing food that is as casual as our city, and that is the kind of food you'll find in this book: simple and delicious.

Choosing the recipes was the hardest part. What you see here is only a highlight of Rio's best, but if you visit me in my Rio or Connecticut kitchen, these are the recipes I would prepare for dinner.

Rio is my foundation; it defines me as a person. I think of all the foods I ate at home growing up like Arroz de Forno (page 189) or my aunt's Moroccan meatballs (page 182), and the memories of my home in Rio come alive. That's why I also included a chapter on home cooking. These recipes are not only part of my memories, they are part of carioca's daily lives.

THE NEIGHBORHOODS

Rio is a very easy city to navigate with the beach as a point of reference. That's why I structured this book by location: each neighborhood with its own personality and my favorite recipes from each.

I focused mostly on the neighborhoods of Zona Sul because that's where I grew up and where the famous neighborhoods like Ipanema, Copacabana, and Leblon are located. It's also where I hunt for recipes and discoveries. But that doesn't mean you should drink a caipirinha only at the Academia da Cachaça, or eat *rissoles de camarão* only at Jobi. On the contrary, you can eat out constantly in Rio, and most of recipes found in this book can be found pretty much all over town, way beyond Zona Sul. Be aware though that, as in any metropolitan city, things change fast, with places opening and closing, restaurants changing addresses and opening other branches. It happens all the time in Rio!

Most of the restaurants featured in this book have been in business for a steady chunk of time, like Terzeto, Olympe, Antiquarius, Jobi, and many others—and I include addresses and websites, when available, for every restaurant mentioned in this book. I am sure by the time this book comes out, however, even more new restaurants will be opening (enticing me with a taste for more!).

My hope is that these recipes can serve as a guide for you to understand the culinary dynamics of Rio, but most importantly that your own cooking will blossom with the use of this book.

I love the rhythm of Rio, the passion, the electricity, the music, and most importantly, the way people cook. The incredibly talented people featured in this book are making Rio a very special place to eat today. Unquestionably, Rio is a global tourist destination. I hope that this book proves that Rio is not just about the carnival, beach, soccer, and music. It's about the food as well. And I hope that this book will endure past the upcoming big events—as the recipes are as timeless as the city itself.

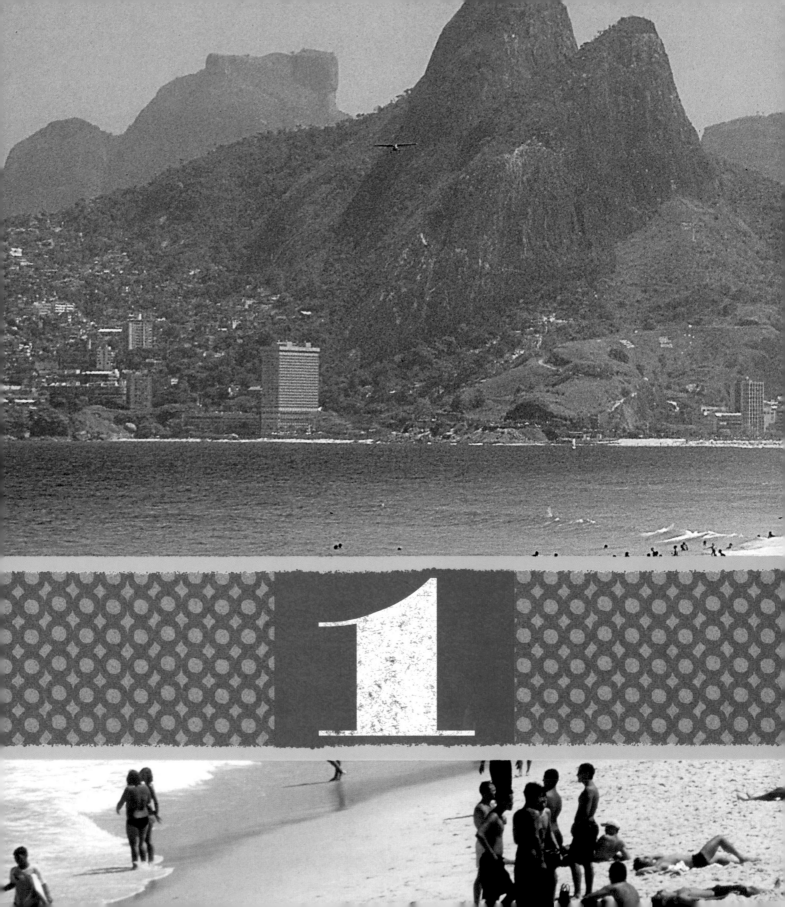

1

THE SPIRIT OF BOTEQUIMS

A *botequim* is a simple type of restaurant that came into being in Brazil in the late 1800s by and for Portuguese immigrants—a place where they could meet, unwind, eat *petiscos* (finger food), and drink, but mostly to take a break from home and work.

The staff typically consists of veteran Portuguese waiters who often have been in the business for just about their whole lives. Today they are as much a part of the scene as the food. The menus are usually written on chalkboards, the tables are squeaky, and the chairs are bare. But the atmosphere is mystical. Ideas, conversations, friendship, and music tend to flow through the tables of botequims in a way unlike anywhere else.

You see people in their twenties, in their eighties, and everyone in between, but most of the regulars who gravitate toward botequims are artists and musicians.

"The Girl from Ipanema" was written by Vinícius de Moraes and Antônio Carlos Jobim while the two were sitting at a botequim in Ipanema at the corners of Prudente de Moraes and Vinícious de Moraes streets enjoying

their caipirinhas. Like the girl from Ipanema, whose walk is more than a swing, a botequim is more than a restaurant. The melody in your mind can be happy or sad; whatever mood you're in, the botequim will likely soothe your soul.

Perhaps the most noteworthy virtue of a botequim is that it is an extension of the beach, bringing people together beyond differences of class, race, and occupation.

I cannot think of Rio without botequims. They are part of our culture and part of our spirit. And no matter how trendy we aspire to be, how vogue the food culture becomes, the botequim is the essential bridge between past and present, nature and culture, food and music, and Portuguese influence and Brazilian habits.

Caipirinha
SUGAR AND LIME COCKTAIL

RESTAURANT: Academia da Cachaça
R. Conde Bernadotte, 26 – Leblon
academiadacachaca.com.br

Of all things Brazilian, you've probably heard of the caipirinha, our heraldic emblem and one of Brazil's greatest contributions to the food and wine world. The spirit behind it, *cachaça*, was invented in the mid-1500s in Brazil when Portuguese colonizers began to cultivate sugarcane. Somewhere in a sugar mill around São Paulo, some stems of rough sugarcane were forgotten, left to sit around, and fermented into a foamy juice. The drink, though non-alcoholic, had a strong effect on the body and was used as a painkiller.

Eventually the Portuguese decided to distill and age it, creating a new type of *aguardente* (spirit distilled from fruits or vegetables) and named it cachaça. There are many different kinds of wood (oak, cherry, and jequitibá rosa among them) used for aging the spirit, each leaving different traces of taste, some with a floral flavor, others with a hint of vanilla or cinnamon.

Cachaça was considered a poor man's drink, and a disdain for it lingered for quite some time. But in Brazil there is a current wave of "waking up" to our own cuisine and ingredients; the culture has changed, and today cachaça couldn't be more in style and caipirinhas have found a global audience.

In the United States cachaça is also called Brazilian rum, and the distillation process is quite similar. The difference between the two is that rum is distilled from molasses (which also comes from sugarcane), while cachaça is distilled from fresh sugarcane juice. Good cachaça has an intense aroma and the flavor of fresh sugarcane.

If you would like to sniff deeper and choose from a selection of hundreds of different cachaças, step off of the beach for an afternoon and visit Academia da Cachaça, a rickety bar devoted entirely to the spirit. You can taste cachaça until you end up under the table, or you can do what I do: I practice my devotion eating some *petiscos* (bar food) with a caipirinha on the side. The food at Academia da Cachaça is just as amazing as the caipirinhas.

SERVES 1

2 limes

1 tablespoon sugar

2 to 3 tablespoons cachaça

Ice cubes

Cut the two ends off the lime and cut the lime into medium wedges.

Using a muddler, mash the lime with the sugar, making sure to squeeze out all the juice and to dissolve the sugar in the juice.

Transfer the lime mixture to a shaker. Add the cachaça and ice cubes, shake well (8 to 10 times), and pour into a large (but not tall), sturdy glass.

Serve immediately.

Suco de Mamâo com Laranja
PAPAYA AND ORANGE SMOOTHIE

Papaya is tropical, bright, and buttery with a complex sweetness. The fruit pairs particularly nicely with the tang of orange. As a child, this smoothie was the first one I liked at BB Lanches, a juice store in Leblon. It is a classic juice bar offering, and I make it all the time for breakfast in my own kitchen, especially when I can find papayas from Brazil. Papayas are so sweet that this smoothie doesn't call for any added sugar, but if you like yours a little sweeter, feel free to add a dash of sugar or other sweetener.

SERVES 1

1 small papaya, seeded and peeled

1 cup fresh orange juice (from about 2 oranges)

Combine the papaya and orange juice in a blender and blend for about 2 minutes, until completely smooth.

Pour into a tall highball glass and serve immediately.

. . . .
RESTAURANT: BB Lanches
R. Aristides Espínola, 64 –
Leblon
. . . .

Rissoles de Camarão Com Catupiry

SHRIMP AND CATUPIRY CHEESE TURNOVERS

RESTAURANT: Bar e Restaurante Jobi, Av. Ataulfo de Paiva, 1166 – Leblon

Located at a perfect corner of Leblon, and just steps from my family home in Rio, Jobi represents the quintessential carioca spirit. For more than fifty years, this botequim has been enchanting the city with its impeccable Portuguese cuisine, prepared in a tiny kitchen that serves extraordinary food. An order of their rissoles comes in a small tray with six turnovers and is one of the things I miss most about my life in Rio. When I go back to visit, my mother always suggests that we go to Jobi on the pretext that it is conveniently located close to our house, but in reality she is totally addicted to these rissoles. And I am too!

MAKES ABOUT 35

DOUGH

2 cups whole milk

3 tablespoons unsalted butter

1½ teaspoons salt

2 cups all-purpose flour, sifted

FILLING

2 tablespoons olive oil

½ pound medium shrimp, peeled and deveined

Kosher salt and freshly ground black pepper

2 tablespoons unsalted butter

1 shallot, minced

1 garlic clove, minced

1 tablespoon all-purpose flour, plus more for dusting

¾ cup whole milk

Kosher salt and freshly ground pepper

Freshly grated nutmeg

½ cup Catupiry cheese, at room temperature

2 cups vegetable oil for frying

2 large eggs, lightly beaten

2 cups plain breadcrumbs

Prepare the dough: In a medium saucepan, combine the milk, butter, and salt and bring to a boil. Add the flour in one stroke and cook, mixing with a wooden spoon, until it releases from the pan, about 3 minutes. Transfer the dough to a lightly floured surface and let rest until cool enough to handle, about 10 minutes. Gather the dough into a ball and knead lightly by hand until it is smooth. Divide the ball in half and flatten each half into a disk. Let cool completely, then wrap each disk lightly with plastic wrap. Do not chill.

Prepare the filling: In a medium skillet, heat the olive oil over medium heat. Season the shrimp with salt and pepper, add them to the skillet, and cook until they just start to turn orange, about 1 minute per side. Transfer to a cutting board, let cool for a few minutes, then roughly chop them (each shrimp should be cut into 4 or 5 pieces). Place into a bowl and cover lightly with foil.

In the same skillet, melt the butter over low heat, add the shallots, and cook until softened and translucent, about 2 minutes. Add the garlic and cook until softened, about another minute. Add the flour and stir with a wooden spoon, making sure everything blends together without browning. Add the milk and stir constantly until the mixture thickens, about 3 minutes. Season with salt, pepper, and nutmeg. Pour into the bowl with the shrimp and fold everything together. Taste, adjust the seasonings, and cool completely.

Have a small bowl of water and a pastry brush on hand. Place one disk of dough on a lightly floured surface and dust with flour. Roll into a 1/16-inch-thick oval. Using a 3½-inch round cookie cutter, cut out as many circles as you can get. (You can gather the scraps and knead again, but note that this dough can easily be overkneaded, so go gently and take care to prevent cracks from appearing.)

Place 1 tablespoon of the shrimp filling onto each dough circle and spread 1 teaspoon of cheese on top. Brush a bit of water around the edges and fold each circle in half, pressing the edges with your fingers to seal tightly. Repeat with the rest of the dough and filling. (At this point you can refrigerate the rissoles in a plastic container for up to 2 days.)

Pour the vegetable oil into a heavy-bottomed pot and heat to 350°F as measured by a deep-fat thermometer.

Prepare three different shallow bowls: one for the eggs, one for the breadcrumbs, and one for the assembled rissoles. Dip each rissole into the egg and transfer to the breadcrumbs, coating well. (I like to keep one hand wet for the eggs and the other hand dry for the breadcrumbs.)

Fry the rissoles in batches, adding as many as will fit without touching and turning them with a long slotted spoon so they brown evenly on all sides. Transfer to a plate lined with paper towels. Continue working in batches until all the rissoles are fried. Serve immediately. (You can keep the rissoles in a plastic container in the fridge for up to 3 days and reheat in a 300°F oven for 5 to 10 minutes.)

Bolinho de Bacalhau
GOLDEN SALT COD FRITTERS

These addictive fried treats are one of Rio's greatest gustatory experiences, and you can find them in just about every botequim in the city in many variations. But they have a very special meaning for Chico & Alaíde. After working at Bracarense (another fantastic botequim worth visiting) for fifteen years—he as a waiter, she as a cook—Chico and Alaíde gathered their savings, rolled up their sleeves, and opened this excellent botequim, doing exactly what they do best: serving and cooking bar food. It is the first of many restaurants that line Rua Dias Ferreira, one of the most buzzed about streets in Rio. The ambience is slightly more polished than an old timer, reflecting the young age of this botequim. Creativity runs wild through Alaíde's veins, but I still love the traditional *bolinho de bacalhau*, a recipe that is just as much a part of their journey as it is part of Rio's history.

MAKES ABOUT 115

2 pounds salt cod

3 cups cold milk

5 large russet potatoes (about 3 lbs)

Kosher salt

1 tablespoon olive oil

2 garlic cloves, minced

1 medium shallot, minced

6 large egg yolks

2 tablespoons freshly chopped parsley

Cayenne pepper

Freshly ground black pepper

Freshly grated nutmeg

2 cups vegetable or canola oil for frying

RESTAURANT: Chico e Alaíde,
Rua Dias Ferreira, 679 – Leblon
chicoealaide.com.br

Rinse the cod in cold water and place it in a large container. (The volume of water should be 10 to 15 times the size of the cod, so use a very big container; you can cut the fish to fit the container if necessary.) Cover with cold water, cover with a tight-fitting lid, and soak in the refrigerator for 12 to 24 hours, changing the water at least 3 times. Drain.

Transfer the cod to a medium saucepan and cover with the milk. Bring to a boil over medium heat, then reduce the heat to low and cook until the cod until becomes opaque, about 20 minutes. Turn off the heat and let cool.

When cool enough to handle, use a slotted spoon to remove the cod and discard the milk. Flake the cod with your hands into big chunks, then shred it by either chopping with a chef's knife or pulsing in a food processor. The fish will have lost about half its weight at this point: expect about 1½ pounds (4½ cups) of shredded fish. You can now place the cod in a storage container, cover with a tight-fitting lid, and refrigerate for up to 6 hours, until ready to use.

Peel the potatoes and chop them. Place in a heavy-bottomed saucepan and add cold water to cover and a pinch of salt. Cover the pan, bring to a boil, then reduce the heat to medium and simmer until the potatoes are fork-tender, 8 to 10 minutes. Drain, and while still hot, pass the potatoes through a ricer or food mill—you will have 5 to 6 cups of mashed potatoes. Assemble the cod fritters while the potatoes are still warm.

In a large bowl, combine the shredded cod and mashed potatoes. Add the olive oil, garlic, shallot, egg yolks, and parsley. If the batter gets too difficult to mix by hand, you can use an electric mixer fitted with the paddle attachment at low speed. Season with cayenne, salt, pepper, and nutmeg.

Preheat the oven to 200°F.

Roll the mixture into 1-inch balls, place them on baking sheets, and refrigerate for 30 minutes while you prepare the oil for frying.

Pour the vegetable oil into a heavy-bottomed saucepan and heat it to 350°F, as measured by a deep-fat thermometer. Drop in 12 to 14 cod balls—only as many as will fit without touching each other. Fry, turning occasionally with a long slotted spoon, making sure both sides are browned evenly, about 5 minutes. Transfer to a baking sheet lined with paper towels. Continue working in batches until all the fritters are fried; keep the finished batches in the oven as you go. When all the fritters are fried, serve immediately.

INGREDIENT NOTE: When buying salt cod, look for a piece that's very meaty and trim off the dark parts around the belly and tail before soaking.

Salada de Bacalhau, Feijão Branco, e Cebola Roxa

SALT COD AND WHITE BEAN SALAD WITH RED ONIONS

Tapas in Spain, petiscos in Brazil: the two have a lot in common. Venga is one of the few botequims that has embraced the spirit of Rio with a Spanish influence. Before it opened its doors in 2009, Fernando Kaplan, one of the partners, traveled to Spain to research the world of tapas, and the result is simply terrific: Spain on a plate as seen from Rio de Janeiro. The restaurant is charming, thanks to a world of bottles decorating the walls, and a setup of bar tables, standard dining tables, and communal tables add to the atmosphere; conversations sparkle and flow while you wait for the food to arrive. This recipe is inspired by a delicious salad I ate there, a perfect meeting of carioca and Spanish cuisines.

SERVES 6-8

1 pound dry white beans such as Cannellini or Great Northern, picked and rinsed

1 large red onion, cut in half and thinly sliced

1 tablespoon sherry vinegar

½ teaspoon salt

2 tablespoons olive oil

2¼ pounds salt cod, soaked, drained, and cooked (see page 20 for instructions)

¼ cup fresh chopped parsley

DRESSING

Juice of ½ lime

2 tablespoons sherry vinegar

1 small garlic clove, mashed into a paste

Tabasco sauce

½ cup olive oil, plus more for drizzling

Place the beans in a large saucepan or pressure cooker. Add about 2 quarts water, cover the pan or lock the pressure cooker, and cook until the beans are cooked but not mushy (about 1½ hours for a saucepan, 30 minutes for a pressure cooker). Drain and discard the water. Spread the beans on a large plate to cool.

Put the onion slices in a bowl and add enough water to cover, about 1 cup. Add the vinegar and salt and let sit for 40 minutes.

Drain the onions and discard the water. In a small skillet, heat the olive oil over low heat; add the onions and cook until softened, about 6 minutes, stirring frequently. They will remain bright red—that's what you want. Transfer to a plate and cool.

Roughly chop the salt cod, then shred with your fingers, discarding any fatty or dark pieces.

Make the dressing: Combine the lime juice, vinegar, garlic, and a few drops of Tabasco in a small bowl, then add the olive oil in a steady stream, whisking constantly until emulsified.

Place the beans and cod in a bowl. Add the red onions and parsley. Pour the dressing over and mix well with a rubber spatula. Taste and adjust the seasoning with salt and pepper. Cover and refrigerate for at least 2 hours to develop the flavors. Bring to room temperature 30 minutes before serving.

COOKING TIP: I prefer to cook dry white beans, but you can use canned beans to save time.

RESTAURANT: Venga, R. Dias Ferreira, 113 – Leblon
venga.com.br

Frango à Passarinho
BRAZILIAN-STYLE FRIED CHICKEN

Frango à passarinho translates to "chicken bird style," referring to the small pieces the chicken is cut into. This dish is inspired by Bracarense, an iconic botequim, and any home cook can handle this simple recipe. It's fried chicken at its most basic—golden and crunchy, garnished with sliced or chopped garlic and fresh parsley. I often make it in my American kitchen for my family when I am looking for a way to add a Brazilian twist to a chicken dish, and then my kids add their own American twist by dipping it in a side of barbecue sauce. Between one twist and another, an amazing dinner is the result, and the platter goes back to the kitchen absolutely clean.

SERVES 6–8 AS AN APPETIZER OR 4 AS A MAIN COURSE

1 whole chicken (3 to 4 pounds)

1 teaspoon finely grated lime zest

4 tablespoons fresh lime juice

One 350ml bottle of beer, like Stella Artois

2 cups canola or vegetable oil for frying

Kosher salt and freshly ground black pepper

1 cup all-purpose flour

4 to 5 garlic cloves, thinly sliced or roughly chopped

3 tablespoons chopped fresh parsley

Remove the skin from the chicken and cut it into 2-inch pieces. Place in a bowl and add the lime zest, lime juice, and beer. Cover with plastic wrap and marinate for 1 hour at room temperature. Drain the chicken, discarding the liquid, and spread the chicken pieces on a baking sheet lined with paper towels. Air-dry for at least 5 minutes. It's okay if some of the lime zest remains on the chicken.

In a deep, wide skillet, heat the oil over medium heat until it registers 350°F on a deep-fry thermometer.

Season the chicken with salt and pepper on all sides. Place the flour in a large, shallow bowl and season with salt and pepper. Roll the chicken pieces in the flour, shake off some but not all of the excess flour, and arrange the pieces on a baking sheet.

Working in batches, add the chicken pieces one at a time to the oil, only putting in as many as will fit in the pan without touching, and turn the chicken with tongs so it's golden on all sides, about 8 minutes for each batch.

Transfer the chicken pieces to a baking sheet lined with paper towels.

Quickly add the garlic to same oil in the pan and fry, stirring constantly, until it just starts to turn golden, about 2 minutes. Remove the garlic from the oil with a slotted spoon, sprinkle the garlic over the chicken, and finish with the parsley. Serve immediately.

RESTAURANT: Bar Bracarense,
Rua Jose Linhares,
85 – Leblon

Bacalhau à Gomes Sá
BAKED SALT COD WITH POTATOES, ONIONS, EGGS, AND OLIVES

Dinner at Antiquarius serves rustic Portuguese cuisine at a sophisticated level, with dishes that are based on tradition and service that is deeply personalized. When visiting Antiquarius, ask to meet Manuel Pires, or Manuelzinho, one of the most beloved waiters in all of Rio. His descriptions of their cod dishes are mouthwatering, and *bacalhau à Gomes Sá* is a highlight on the menu. The name of this dish comes from a cook named José Luiz Gomes de Sá, who created this recipe in the early 1900s while working at a restaurant in the city of Porto, Portugal. The dish was brought to Brazil by Portuguese immigrants and today is one of the most well-known cod recipes in both countries.

SERVES 8–10

2 pounds salt cod, soaked, drained, and cooked (see page 20 for instructions)

2½ cups cold milk

2 pounds small new or Yukon gold potatoes, halved and sliced ¾-inch thick

Kosher salt

1¼ cups plus 3 tablespoons extra virgin olive oil

3 medium onions, thinly sliced

¼ cup chopped fresh parsley

Freshly ground black pepper

3 hard-boiled eggs, thinly sliced

¼ cup kalamata olives, pitted and halved

RESTAURANT: Antiquarius,
R. Aristides Espínola,
19 – Leblon

Preheat the oven to 350°F. Lightly coat a 9 x 13-inch baking dish with cooking spray.

Place the salt cod in a medium saucepan, cutting the fish to fit the pan if necessary. Cover the salt cod with the milk. Bring to a boil over high heat, then reduce the heat to low and cook, covered, until the salt cod becomes opaque, about 15 minutes. Turn the heat off and let the salt cod rest, covered, in the milk for at least 20 minutes. Using a slotted spoon, remove the salt cod and discard the milk. Flake the fish with your hands into small chunks or pulse it in a food processor for just a few seconds. Place the salt cod in a storage container, cover with a tight-fitting lid, and refrigerate for up to 6 hours, until ready to use.

Place the potatoes in a large heavy saucepan. Cover with cold water by at least 1 inch and add a large pinch of salt. Bring to a boil over high heat, then reduce the heat to medium and simmer until fork-tender, 12 to 15 minutes. Drain, then spread the potatoes over a plate. Set aside.

Heat 3 tablespoons of the olive oil in a large skillet over low heat. Add the onions and cook, stirring occasionally, until softened and translucent, 15 to 20 minutes. Resist the temptation to use high heat to avoid browning them. If they do begin to brown, add a tablespoon of water. In a large bowl, combine the shredded salt cod, onions, and potatoes. Mix in ¼ cup of the remaining olive oil and the parsley. Taste, and season lightly with salt (the cod will already be salty) and pepper.

Spread the mixture evenly across the prepared baking dish. Drizzle the remaining 1 cup olive oil over the top. Place in the oven and bake until bubbling hot, 15 to 20 minutes. Remove the dish from the oven, distribute the eggs and olives all over, and return the dish to the oven for another 10 minutes to heat through. Serve hot.

INGREDIENT NOTE: When buying salt cod, look for a piece that looks very meaty and trim away the dark parts around the belly and tail before soaking.

Dadinhos de Tapioca com Queijo
CRISPY TAPIOCA CHEESE FRITTERS

Zuka is a very versatile restaurant: whatever purpose—business lunch, romantic date, dinner with friends—it fits the occasion. The menu sprinkles exotic Brazilian ingredients with dishes that are internationally familiar. I was interviewing Chef Ludmilla Soeiro for my blog when I first tried these crunchy tapioca fritters. I couldn't get over how remarkably delicious they were and couldn't wait to try the recipe at home. I made them with Parmesan, cured and grated Minas cheese, Brazilian coalho cheese, and Greek haloumi. My favorite is Parmesan, but they all produce a great fritter. Ludmilla told me that she learned this recipe from Chef Rodrigo Oliveira, based in São Paulo—(see page 127 for another of his recipes)—proving that good recipes travel fast.

MAKES ABOUT 45

1⅓ cups finely grated fresh Parmesan

½ cup plus 1 tablespoon small tapioca pearls

1 cup whole milk

Kosher salt and freshly ground black pepper

Freshly grated nutmeg

Pinch of paprika

2 cups vegetable oil for frying

Line a small (1-quart) baking dish with plastic wrap, leaving an overhang on all sides. Be sure it's deep enough to hold the batter.

In a medium bowl, combine the cheese and tapioca. In a small saucepan, bring the milk to a boil. Pour the hot milk over the tapioca and mix with a rubber spatula; the tapioca will immediately start to release starch and the dough will become thick and pasty. Season with salt, pepper, nutmeg, and paprika. Pour into the prepared baking dish and spread evenly. Immediately cover with plastic wrap to prevent a skin from forming. Let cool at room temperature for at least 1 hour, then refrigerate for at least 2 hours or up to 5 days.

Pour the vegetable oil into a heavy-bottomed saucepan and heat to 350°F, as measured by a deep-fat thermometer.

Unmold the tapioca dough onto a cutting board. Using a long knife, trim the edges and cut the dough into neat 1-inch cubes.

Fry the tapioca cubes in batches, adding only as many as will fit without touching. Turn occasionally with a long slotted spoon, preventing them from sticking together, until evenly browned on all sides, about 3 minutes. Transfer to a baking sheet lined with paper towels. Continue working in batches until all the fritters are fried. Serve immediately.

RESTAURANT: Zuka,
R. Dias Ferreira, 233 – Leblon
zuka.com.br

COOKING TIP: You can bake these in a 350°F oven for 12 to 15 minutes, but frying brings the best crispness to the plate. Serve them with red pepper jam on the side if you like.

INGREDIENT NOTE: If you can get your hands on the Brazilian tapioca flour from Yoki or Bascom's, which you can easily find on Amazon, use it instead of the tapioca pearls and these will taste ultra-extraordinaire.

Brigadeiro
SWEET MILK AND CHOCOLATE FUDGE

This iconic Brazilian sweet was named after Eduardo Gomes, a brigadier who, in the early 1900s, was admired for his good looks and notoriously loved chocolate. When sweetened condensed milk was invented (in Switzerland) and brought to Brazil, chefs created this fudge using the sweet milk and chocolate. This recipe is inspired by the brigadeiro sold at Colher de Pau. Eating their sweets is a journey into the past, and Colher de Pau is a landmark in Rio. Thirty-something years have passed, and the brigadeiro of my childhood is still there, as fudgy, handsome, and seducing as ever.

MAKES ABOUT 20

One 14–ounce can sweetened condensed milk

1 tablespoon unsalted butter

6 tablespoons unsweetened cocoa powder (preferably Giardelli)

½ cup chocolate sprinkles

RESTAURANT: Colher de Pau
R. Rita Ludolf, 90 – Leblon
colherdepaurio.com.br

In a medium heavy-bottomed saucepan, combine the condensed milk, butter, and cocoa powder. Place over medium heat and bring to a boil. Reduce the heat to low and cook, stirring constantly with a wooden spoon, until the mixture is thick and creamy, 8 to 10 minutes. You'll know it's ready when you swirl the pan around and the whole mixture slides as one soft piece and leaves a thick residue on the bottom of the pan.

Slide the mixture into a bowl. Don't scrape the pan—you don't want to include any of the burnt batter that stayed on the bottom of the pan. Cool to room temperature, then cover and refrigerate for at least 4 hours, or preferably overnight.

Scoop the mixture by the teaspoonful and, using your hands, roll it into little balls about ¾ inch in diameter.

Place the sprinkles in a shallow dish. Pass the brigadeiros, 4 to 6 at a time, through the sprinkles, making sure they stick and cover the entire surface. Eat immediately or store in an airtight container for up to 3 days, after which the condensed milk will crystallize (making a crunchier brigadeiro that is still okay to eat).

Toalha Felpuda
COCONUT LAYER CAKE WITH COCONUT PASTRY CREAM AND MERINGUE FROSTING

This coconut cake is based on the one you'll find at Colher de Pau (see box on page 27), a sweet little store in Leblon. The translation of *toalha felpuda* is "furry towel," referring to the white blanket of coconut frosting that covers the cake. From the very first bite, you'll recognize that this is a coconut cake unlike any other. There is something about it that allows you to eat without feeling the weight of food entering your body, as if you were eating coconut clouds. That's because there is no flour—only potato starch—and no butter in the frosting. Both the pastry cream and the cake benefit from chilling time before assembling; the pastry cream could even be made the day before and refrigerated overnight.

SERVES 8–10

6 large eggs, separated, at room temperature

2 large egg yolks, at room temperature

1½ cups sugar

Salt

1¾ cups potato starch, sifted

COCONUT PASTRY CREAM

3 large egg yolks

5 tablespoons sugar

2 tablespoons cornstarch

1⅔ cups coconut milk

2 tablespoons unsalted butter, at room temperature

½ cup plus 2 tablespoons heavy cream

¾ cup fresh or dried grated coconut

COCONUT MERINGUE

6 large egg whites

1½ cups sugar

1 teaspoon vanilla extract

1½ cups coconut milk, brought to a light boil then cooled

1½ cups unsweetened grated coconut, preferably fresh

Set an oven rack in the middle position and preheat the oven to 350°F. Butter a 10 x 2-inch round cake pan, line the bottom with parchment paper, butter the paper, and dust with flour, shaking off excess.

Make the cake: In the bowl of an electric mixer fitted with the whisk attachment, beat all 8 egg yolks with ½ cup of the sugar until the mixture thickens and turns pale yellow.

In a separate bowl, beat the 6 egg whites with a pinch of salt on medium speed until frothy. With the mixer running, gradually sprinkle the remaining 1 cup sugar and beat until soft peaks forms.

Using a rubber spatula, fold one third of the egg whites into the egg yolk mixture, then fold in the remaining egg whites. Slowly sprinkle the potato starch over the mixture and fold carefully with a rubber spatula, scraping all the way to the bottom of the bowl on every pass to prevent the potato starch from accumulating or forming lumps.

Scrape the batter into the prepared cake pan and smooth the top with an offset spatula. Bake, rotating the pan halfway through, until a cake tester inserted into the center comes out clean, 40 to 45 minutes.

Let cool in the pan on a wire rack for 30 minutes, then turn the cake out and let it cool completely on the rack. Cover the cake loosely with plastic wrap and refrigerate for at least 5 hours.

Make the coconut pastry cream: In a medium bowl, whisk together the egg yolks, 3 tablespoons of the sugar, and the cornstarch.

In a medium saucepan, bring the coconut milk to a simmer over medium heat. Whisking constantly, pour the hot coconut milk into the egg yolk mixture, gradually at first to temper it, and then more quickly. Transfer the mixture back to the saucepan and cook over low heat, whisking constantly, until it reaches a pudding-like consistency, about 4 minutes. Transfer to a bowl and let sit for 10 minutes, stirring occasionally. Whisk in the butter.

In the bowl of an electric mixer fitted with the whisk attachment, whip the heavy cream with the remaining 2 tablespoons sugar until fluffy. Fold it into the coconut pastry cream, then fold in the grated coconut. Press a piece of plastic wrap directly over the cream to prevent a crust

INGREDIENT NOTES:
The coconut used in the pastry cream can be dried, but try to use freshly grated coconut to cover the cake. It makes a big difference!

Different brands of potato starch vary in weight, so if you have a scale, use it to measure the amount of grams for greatest accuracy. I use Ener-G potato starch.

.

from forming and refrigerate until firm, for at least 2 hours or preferably overnight.

Make the coconut meringue: Combine the egg whites and sugar in the bowl of an electric mixer and set it over a pot of simmering water (the bowl should not touch the water). Whisk constantly until the mixture is warm to the touch and slightly foamy and the sugar is completely dissolved. Remove the bowl from the pot and set it on the base of the mixer fitted with the whisk attachment; whip on medium-high speed until the mixture is fluffy, glossy, and completely cooled, about 10 minutes. Whisk in the vanilla.

To assemble the cake, use a long serrated knife to trim the top and sides of the cake, then cut the cake into 3 equal horizontal layers. Set one layer cut side up on a cardboard disk and brush generously with the coconut milk. Spread half of the coconut pastry cream over the cake with an offset spatula. Top with another cake layer, brush with coconut milk, and spread the remaining coconut pastry cream on top. Set the third cake layer on top, cut side down, and frost the sides and top of the cake with the coconut meringue. Gently pat the grated coconut all over the cake.

PANEMA

A TRIBUTE TO THE FARMERS' MARKET

When I am in Rio, I spend a lot of time browsing the city's many food markets. Not just the street markets that are found each day in a different Zona Sul neighborhood, but also the fish market in Niterói, the Feira de São Cristovão, and Cadeg in Benfica.

To me these markets are some of the most enlightening, energizing, and generous places in the world

When I was a kid, I would join my mother at the gym in Ipanema, and we would always make a stop at the same farmers' market on Fridays. I remember that "aha!" moment when I realized that the orange roulade, a treat I was crazy for, was actually prepared by the Portuguese lady behind the stand. I am still crazy for it, and you can try my version in this chapter. As a young teenager attracted by anything edible, I took over the role of going to the market for my mother, whose favorite part of the market was the flower stand; we never had an official agreement, but as my mother saw my growing enthusiasm for food, she eventually passed the baton to me.

But it wasn't until my late teenage years, when I started cooking more seriously, that I really became a market aficionada. Where else could I learn about salt cod or bond with a lady over a shared love of orange roulade? When I want to learn about new ingredients, the first thing I do is go to the market to figure out what am I going to prepare and how to cook it.

I also enjoy the characters and personalities. The shouting, the tastings,

the way a produce vendor cuts a mango or a melon to entice you to buy his or her fruits and vegetables. Each vendor represents a different face of Brazil: the cupuaçú, which comes from the Amazon, is sold by a native Amazonian; the salt cod by a Portuguese; and the dendê (palm) oil by an African-Brazilian. Between the laughter of the vendors and the chaos of the cariocas rushing about for the freshest ingredients, you leave the market with a sense that Rio is the most magical of cities.

Over the years I have learned that there is no tradition of sharing recipes in Brazil. The recipes are handed down by generation, and people are not about to give their secret recipes away—especially to someone who makes a living from recipe writing. As much as I disagree with this practice, it has forced me to be a better cook as I try to replicate the baked goods I've tasted at the market at home.

Rio's markets are places of hard work and early rising. I have seen men carrying impossibly huge buckets of ice to prepare a nice display of fish, and I have seen women peel and chop piles of vegetables to bag them perfectly. Grating coconut may last all morning long, because no one wants to do this job at home, but much coconut is needed to prepare the coconut-based dishes you'll find at the market. It all starts at the crack of dawn, so that by 7 a.m. everything looks gorgeous.

Rio's markets are also places of beauty. Food and people connect intensely. I see housewives buying produce for the family dinner, and I see beautiful cut-up guavas perfuming the air. I notice the curves of a pumpkin, and it reminds of a woman rolling a wagon full of groceries. I see women coming to the market straight from the gym. I see the wrinkles of a chayote, and those in the eyes of a fisherman. I see colors I didn't know existed, fruit I have never tasted, and people who are as passionate about cooking as I am.

I've learned a lot about life in Rio's markets. Vendors need to sell their items, customers need to buy food, and there is a world of choices at our feet. The markets have taught me how to negotiate for a better price, to choose the best produce, and to wait for the next stand. But mostly the markets have taught me about human relationships.

GREAT MARKETS IN RIO

Farmers' Markets:

Mondays:	Rua Henrique Dumont, Ipanema
Tuesdays:	Praça General Osório, Leblon
Wednesdays:	Rua General San Martin, Leblon
Thursdays:	Aterro do Flamengo, Botafogo
Fridays:	Praça Nossa Senhora da Paz, Ipanema

Feira de São Cristóvão

I vividly remember my first visit to the market in São Cristóvão. I entered by the Luiz Gonzaga statue at the market's entrance, to be drawn into a riot of vivid colors and foods from different regions of Brazil—food that might seem exotic to just about any carioca. Among the many market treasures, I found a stand with more than ten different types of yucca flour.

feiradesaocristovao.org.br

Mercado de Peixes São Pedro in Niterói

Located on the other side of the bridge across from Rio, this fish market is recognized as the most important in the state of Rio de Janeiro. It supplies most restaurants and supermarkets in the region, but it also sells directly to the customer. The building holds more then twenty different stands and several restaurants specializing in fish are located on the second floor. You can buy your own fish downstairs, bring it to a restaurant, and they will prepare it fresh for you. Most of the fish in the market is sold by 2 p.m.

Mercado de Peixes São Pedro, Rua Visconde do Rio Branco, 55, Niterói, Rio de Janeiro
Hours of Operation:
Tuesdays to Saturdays, 6 a.m. to 6 p.m.
Sundays, 6 a.m. to 12 p.m.

Feira Hippie Ipanema

Although this market is mostly about décor, arts, and crafts, there are a few food stands on the corner of Prudente de Moraes Street. My favorite are the Baianas selling *acarajés* (bean fritters).

FeiraHippieIpanema.com

Limonada Suíssa
BRAZILIAN-STYLE LIMEADE

Lemonade is a drink adored in all parts of the world. In the United States lemonade is the quintessential flavor of summer, and if you like it, you will love this Brazilian version made with limes. Aside from its beautiful pastel green color, what I love about this classic Brazilian refreshment is that it makes use of the whole lime, both the juice and peel with all its aromatic oils. I love to order a limonada at Polis Sucos after a visit to the gym.

MAKES 1 TALL GLASS

2 limes

¼ cup sugar

1½ cups water

Ice cubes

RESTAURANT: Polis Sucos
R. Maria Quitéria,
70 – Rio de Janeiro

Remove both the ends of the limes and cut each lime into eighths. Place in a blender, add the sugar and water, and blend until very smooth, 3 to 4 minutes. Set a fine-mesh strainer over a tall glass and pour in the limeade, pressing the solids against the strainer to extract all the liquid. Discard the solids. Add 2 or 3 ice cubes and serve immediately.

INGREDIENT NOTE: The name of this recipe translates to "Swiss limeade"; this is because the original recipe called for sweetened condensed milk, imported from Switzerland. Today the recipe is prepared with sugar instead.

Biscoito O Globo
YUCCA CRACKER

The story of *biscoito globo* begins in 1953, when the three brothers Ponce (Milton, Jaime, and João) went to live with a cousin who was a baker in São Paulo. Their cousin taught them to make this delicious cracker, which they soon brought to Rio. The cracker went from the aisles of bakeries to the sand of Rio's beaches and there isn't a single carioca who doesn't love yucca crackers. This recipe is inspired by this bland but very addictive cracker. You can make it with vegetable oil or with olive oil. Traditionally the cracker is plump, fluffy, and round—almost the size of an American bagel—but you can also pipe them into sticks, which is easier to do at home as it prevents the crackers from expanding into one big mass.

MAKES ABOUT 60

2⅓ cups sour manioc starch (*povilho azedo*)

1 tablespoon kosher salt

⅓ cup vegetable oil

½ cup whole milk

1 egg

Preheat the oven to 350°F. Line two baking sheets with parchment paper or a silicone mat.

Place the manioc starch in the bowl of an electric mixer. Add the salt and ½ cup of water and break the starch up with your fingers. In a small saucepan, bring another ½ cup of water and the oil to a boil. Immediately pour the hot liquid over the manioc starch and turn the machine on low speed. Beat until the mixture looks like a coarse meal, about 1 minute.

Slowly pour in the milk. Add the egg and beat until the dough turns pale and creamy, 3 to 4 minutes.

Stop the machine and scrape the dough into a pastry bag fitted with a plain round tip, size number 6. Pipe the batter into sticks, leaving about ½ inch between each cracker.

Bake for 25 to 35 minutes, until the crackers rise and are slightly golden. Turn off the heat and leave them in the oven with the door ajar for 30 minutes.

Remove them from the oven and cool completely before serving.

Pão de Queijo
PARMESAN CHEESE ROLLS

RESTAURANT: Esplanada Grill,
R. Barão da Torre, 600 – Ipanema
esplanadagrill.com.br

I'll never forget the first time I ate ostrich. It was at Esplanada Grill, located in the gleaming corner of Rua Barão da Torre and Anibal de Mendonca. The meat was gamey, soft, and juicy, sealing my taste for wild meats that day. Esplanada Grill doesn't look like your typical churrascaria—because it's not. Esplanada Grill built its reputation out of a fine à la carte menu serving exquisite Brazilian beef as well as exotic meats such as *javali* (wild boar), *pirarucu* (a fish from the Amazon River), and the above-mentioned ostrich. But one of my favorite treats at Esplanada is the *pão de queijo*. It is so cheesy that I sometimes find it impossible to save room to appreciate some of the best meat in Rio.

Much has been made of Brazilians' fascination with *pão de queijo*. From Belém do Pará in the north of the country to Rio Grande do Sul in the south, and anywhere in between, *pão de queijo* has the power to ignite conversations and direct dinner choices. This dish is the result of yucca alchemy—a golf ball-size little roll that is chewy, cheesy, and steamy, almost succulent—and it's quite difficult to eat just one.

MAKES 35

3½ cups sour manioc starch
  (*polvilho azedo*)

1 cup water

1 cup whole milk

¾ cup vegetable or canola oil

2 teaspoons salt

3 large eggs

1½ cups finely grated
  Parmesan

Freshly grated nutmeg

⅛ teaspoon cayenne
  pepper

Freshly ground black pepper

INGREDIENT NOTE: The main ingredient in *pão de queijo* is *polvilho azedo*, or sour manioc starch, see the Glossary on page 196. I use Yoki brand, which is easily available online.

Place the manioc starch in the bowl of an electric mixer fitted with the paddle attachment. Set aside.

Combine the water, milk, oil, and salt in a small saucepan and bring to a boil. In one stroke, immediately pour the hot liquid mixture into the manioc starch and turn the machine to low speed. Mix until the dough is smooth and the starch is incorporated, about 2 minutes. Pause the machine and add the eggs. Continue to mix at low speed until the dough develops structure and turns pale yellow, about 5 minutes. The dough will be sticky.

Add the cheese and mix until well incorporated. Season with nutmeg, the cayenne, and a few twists of pepper. Transfer the dough to a bowl, cover with plastic wrap, and refrigerate for at least 2 hours.

Preheat the oven to 350°F. Line 2 baking sheets with parchment.

Wet your hands with olive oil or flour your hands with manioc starch. Use an ice cream scooper to make 1-inch balls; roll the balls into shape with your hands. Place the balls on the prepared baking sheets, leaving 1½ to 2 inches between each. (At this point you can store them in a zip-top bag and freeze them for up to 3 months.)

Place the cheese rolls in the oven and bake, rotating the sheets halfway through baking time, until they puff up and are lightly golden brown, 12 to 14 minutes.

Remove the rolls from the oven and place them in a basket lined with a cloth or dishtowel. Serve immediately while they are still at their warmest and chewiest.

Pasteis de Carne
DEEP-FRIED BEEF EMPANADAS

Pasteis (emapanadas) are great any time of day, but in my experience some of the best ones are sold at the farmers' market in Ipanema for lunch, accompanied by a fresh cup of sugarcane juice. These *pasteis* are rectangular in shape and a lot larger than the versions generally made at home or in restaurants, and that is the version I am presenting here. While you can prepare your own pastry dough and roll it into thin disks, I suggest using store-bought pastry disks—as is done in every household in Rio—as it is a lot of work to get the dough as thin as you'll need it for this recipe.

MAKES ABOUT 15

3 tablespoons olive oil

1 small onion, finely chopped

3 scallions, white and green parts, finely chopped

3 garlic cloves, finely minced

1 teaspoon dried oregano

Kosher salt and freshly ground black pepper

¾ pound ground beef chuck

One 14-ounce can whole tomatoes, seeded and chopped (reserve about ½ cup juice)

2 tablespoons chopped fresh parsley

1 package store-bought Massa de pastel (ready-made pastel dough; see Note) or wonton wrappers

3 cups vegetable or canola oil for frying

In a large skillet, heat the olive oil over medium heat. Add the onion and scallions and cook until softened and translucent, about 2 minutes. Stir in the garlic, add the oregano, and season lightly with salt and pepper.

Add the beef and cook, breaking it up with a wooden spoon until no longer pink, about 5 minutes. Add the tomatoes and a ½ cup of their juice. Reduce the heat to low and cook, stirring occasionally, until the liquid is reduced but the mixture is still moist, about 10 minutes. Mix in the fresh parsley. Spread onto a plate to cool completely

Lay out about 5 pieces of dough at a time on a work surface, keeping the thin plastic attached to each layer. Place about 1½ tablespoons of the meat filling onto each piece of dough. Moisten the edges of the disk with water and fold over to form a half moon shape. Crimp tightly with a fork to secure the edges. At this point the plastic will still be around each pastel, keeping it moist. Repeat until the filling and pastry disks are used.

Pour the vegetable oil into a very large heavy-bottomed pot and heat to 350°F, as measured by a deep-fat thermometer. Carefully remove the plastic wrap from each pastel when you are ready to fry. Drop 2 or 3 pasteis in at a time, and use a slotted spoon to baste oil around them constantly so you are frying both sides at the same time. Keep basting and turning until they are light golden brown, about 2 minutes (they will get a little darker as they cool). Transfer to a baking sheet lined with paper towels while you make the remaining batches. Serve immediately.

INGREDIENT NOTE: *Massa de pastel pronta* (ready-made pastel dough) is packaged with either square or round wrappers layered in plastic wrap; you can use either one here. You can find it in Brazilian stores across the United States or online, or you can substitute wonton wrappers and the result will be just as good.

Feijoada
BRAZILIAN BLACK BEAN STEW

There are various theories as to the origin of feijoada. Some believe it was created by African-Brazilians during colonial times using leftovers from animal parts; others believe the dish was inspired by European meat and bean stews; and still others say that feijoada first became popular in the *favelas* (shantytowns) of Rio. Today the origin of feijoada means little to most modern cariocas, but has become a habit on some Saturdays and a desperate craving on others.

Saturdays in Rio were made for feijoada. Every Saturday, Hotel Caesar Park serves a stunning version, with various meats presented in many cauldrons, the clay pots that are just as characteristic of the dish as the dish itself, and which lend an earthy taste to the food.

A feijoada includes everything your mother ever told you to trim from a piece of meat and move to the side of your plate. This is a dish of bold temptation and prompt surrender for carnivores. It's hard to eat with much finesse around glistening pounds of pork butt, ham hocks, pig's ears, and *carne seca* (dried meat). And that's one of the things I love most about this dish: you can see into people's inner personalities when they eat it.

SERVES 8–10

8 ounces carne seca (see Glossary, page 196), optional

1 pound pork shoulder, cut into 2-inch pieces

1 pound fresh pork belly, cut into 2-inch strips

¾ pound smoked ham hock

4 ounces pancetta, cubed

1½ pounds linguiça, chorizo, or other spicy fresh sausage

1 pound dried black beans, picked and rinsed

3 tablespoons olive oil

5 garlic cloves, finely minced

1 large onion, finely diced

2 scallions, white and green parts, chopped

2 fresh bay leaves

Kosher salt and freshly ground black pepper

Cayenne pepper

Paprika

Freshly grated nutmeg

¼ cup chopped fresh cilantro

¼ cup chopped fresh parsley

If using carne seca, rinse it under cold running water, place it in a bowl, cover with water, and refrigerate for 12 to 24 hours, changing the water at least 3 times. Drain the carne seca and discard the water.

Place all the meats in a large pot and add water to cover by 1 inch. Place over high heat and bring to a boil, then reduce the heat to low and simmer for 1 to 1½ hours. The meats will be done at different times; check frequently; and, using a slotted spoon, transfer each meat to a bowl as it's done and cover with foil to keep it moist. You are looking for the meat to be tender, but keep in mind that it will be cooking for another hour or so with the black beans.

Place the beans in a large pot or pressure cooker. Add about 6 quarts of water, cover the pot or lock the pressure cooker, and cook until the beans are cooked through but not mushy (1½ hours for a pot, 30 minutes for a pressure cooker). Reserve the beans and water in the pot.

In a very large pot, heat the olive oil over medium heat, add the garlic, and cook until it just starts to turn golden, about 1 minute. Add the onion and scallions and cook until softened and translucent, about 5 minutes. Add the bay leaves, season with salt, pepper, cayenne, paprika, and nutmeg, and cook until fragrant, about 3 minutes.

Pour the beans and all the liquid into the pot with the vegetables. Add the meats and any juices that have accumulated. Bring to a simmer over low heat and simmer gently, checking frequently, making sure the liquid level is just right, not too soupy, not too dry. Continue cooking until the flavors meld together, 1 to 1½ hours. While the feijoada is cooking, prepare the rice, collard greens, and toasted manioc flour.

Wash the rice in cold water several times going back and forth between a bowl and a colander, until the water becomes fairly clear. Let the rice sit in the colander to air dry for 5 minutes. Heat 2 tablespoons of the olive oil in a medium saucepan over low heat, add the onion, and cook until it just starts to become fragrant, about 2 minutes. Add the

recipe continues overleaf

ACCOMPANIMENTS

2 cups basmati or jasmine rice

5 tablespoons extra virgin olive oil

1 medium onion, finely diced

kosher salt and freshly ground black pepper

1 bunch of collard greens

3 garlic cloves, finely minced

2 tablespoons unsalted butter

1½ cups toasted manioc flour (*farinha de mandioca*)

4 scallions, finely chopped, green parts reserved for garnish

5 navel oranges, peeled and cut into segments, for garnish

COOKING TIP: Feijoada might seem like a lot of work, but this recipe is an easy one—you just add a bunch of meats to a pot, cover with water, and cook for 1 to 1½ hours. At the same time, you have a separate pot of beans cooking, preferably in a pressure cooker. You then combine them to simmer for another 1 to 1½ hours while the meats and beans share flavors. Seasoning the meats a day ahead will give an even greater depth of flavor.

rice and stir with a wooden spoon until the grains are covered in fat and shiny. Add 3 cups water and 2 teaspoons salt and partially cover the pan. Bring to a boil over high heat, then reduce the heat to low and cook until the rice is tender, about 15 minutes.

Trim the stems and thick center ribs from the collard greens and discard them. Stack a few leaves and roll them tightly into a cigar shape. Cut into very thin strips crosswise and place the strips in a bowl. Repeat with the remaining leaves. You should have between 2 and 3 packed cups total. Fill a large saucepan with water and bring it to a boil. Add about 1 tablespoon salt, then add the collard greens and blanch for 30 to 60 seconds, until wilted. Drain, transfer to an ice bath to cool, then drain again.

In a medium saucepan, heat 1 tablespoon of the olive oil over medium heat. Add the garlic and cook until it just starts to turn golden, about 2 minutes. Add the collard greens (you might need to do this in batches) and stir to coat them in the oil. Season with salt and pepper, add about ¼ cup water, and cook until the greens are soft but still bright green, about 3 minutes.

Melt the butter in a medium saucepan over low heat. Add the manioc flour and toast, stirring constantly, until it is a light golden color, 8 to 10 minutes. Watch carefully, as the flour can burn easily. Remove from the heat and set aside.

In a large nonstick skillet, heat the remaining 2 tablespoons olive oil over medium heat. Add the scallions and cook until softened, about 3 minutes. Stir in the toasted manioc flour. Season with salt and pepper, pour into a serving dish, and garnish with the reserved scallions.

Place a mound of rice on a plate, ladle the beans with meats on top. Add the toasted manioc flour and collard greens alongside, and garnish with the fresh cilantro and parsley and navel oranges.

INGREDIENT NOTE: Feijoada is a blank canvas for meat choices—I have never eaten a feijoada in Rio with the same meats. And every time I make feijoada it's a new variation depending on where I am and what market I shop at. Any given feijoada can include four to six types of meat, but you can use more or less depending on what is available. Sometimes I mix pork and beef; other times I stick to pork. When I am in Rio I try to include carne seca (see Glossary, page 196), but in my American kitchen I often skip it because it means a special trip to the Brazilian grocery store.

Risotto de Camarão e Abóbora
SHRIMP AND BUTTERNUT SQUASH RISOTTO

RESTAURANT: Gero
Aníbal de Mendonça
157 – Ipanema

This recipe is inspired by Gero, an Italian restaurant from the Fasano Group that started in São Paulo and opened branches in Rio. The restaurant brings a small slice of Italy to Rio, and this dish features the glory of a creamy risotto mixed with sweetened squash and plump shrimp. You can use chicken stock to prepare this recipe, or you can roast the shells from the cleaned shrimp in a saucepan with an onion, about 2 cloves of garlic, and a tablespoon of tomato paste, simmer for 20 minutes, and call that your shrimp stock.

SERVES 4

6 tablespoons olive oil

3 cups butternut squash, cut into ½-inch dice

Kosher salt and freshly ground black pepper

Freshly grated nutmeg

Ground cinnamon

4 cups chicken stock or shrimp stock (see above)

3 tablespoons unsalted butter

1 medium onion, chopped

1 cup Arborio rice

½ cup dry white wine

1 pound raw medium shrimp, peeled and deveined (about 22 shrimp)

In a medium saucepan, heat 2 tablespoons of the oil over medium heat. Add the squash and cook, stirring frequently with a wooden spoon, until tender, about 15 minutes. Season with salt, pepper, a little nutmeg, and a dash of cinnamon and set aside.

Meanwhile, in a separate medium saucepan, bring the stock to a simmer and keep it there.

In a large, heavy saucepan, melt 1 tablespoon of the butter in 2 tablespoons of the remaining olive oil over medium heat. Add the onion and cook, stirring frequently, until softened and translucent, about 2 minutes. Add the rice and stir frequently until the grains are shiny and coated with the onion mixture, about 3 minutes. Add the wine and bring to a boil; boil until the liquid is almost all absorbed, about 2 minutes.

Slowly add a ladle of simmering stock to the rice and cook, stirring often, until the liquid is absorbed. Adjust the heat to maintain a gentle simmer. Add another ladle and repeat, continuing to add more stock when the previous addition has been completely absorbed. Cook until the rice is tender but still firm to the bite, 18 to 20 minutes, taking care that the risotto doesn't get too thick. If the rice seems to have absorbed all of the liquid and is still too firm, add another tablespoon or so of stock to achieve the right creamy consistency, and taste, checking for flavor and doneness. Season lightly with salt and pepper.

While you are cooking the rice, prepare the shrimp: In a large 12-inch skillet, heat the remaining 2 tablespoons olive oil over medium heat. Season the shrimp with salt and pepper, add them to the skillet, and sauté until they just start to turn orange, about 1 minute per side. Using a slotted spoon, transfer the shrimp to a bowl and cover with foil.

Fold the squash into the rice, then fold in the shrimp. Finish with the remaining 2 tablespoons of butter and serve immediately

Tagliatelle com Camarão, Aspargus, e Leite de Côco do Terzetto

TAGLIATELLE WITH SHRIMP, ASPARAGUS, AND COCONUT MILK

RESTAURANT: Terzetto
R. Jangadeiros, 28
terzetto.com.br

Pasta with shrimp and asparagus is a classic served all over the world—we all know that. But there is nothing common about this dish, a version of which I ate at Terzetto, a traditional Italian restaurant in Rio. The twist—done Brazilian style—is the coconut cream sauce, infusing the shrimp and asparagus with a nutty aroma and richness. I like to make my own shrimp stock by roasting the shells with an onion, about 2 cloves of garlic, and a tablespoon of tomato paste, but any chicken or fish stock will do.

SERVES 4

Kosher salt

8 ounces Italian tagliatelle (or linguine or fettuccini)

8 ounces (about ½ bunch) asparagus, bottoms trimmed

3 tablespoons extra virgin olive oil

1 pound medium shrimp, peeled and deveined

Freshly ground black pepper

1 large shallot, finely minced

1 cup shrimp stock from the shells or chicken stock, plus more for tossing pasta (optional)

1 cup coconut milk, plus more for tossing pasta

2 tablespoons cognac

2 tablespoons chopped fresh chives

Fill a pot with 4 quarts of water and bring to a boil over high heat. Add a large pinch of salt, then add the tagliatelle and stir. Cook, stirring frequently, until the pasta is 2 minutes away from al dente according to the package instructions. Drain the pasta, saving some of the pasta water just in case.

Fill a bowl with ice and water. Place the asparagus in a steamer basket and season with salt. Add a small amount of water to the bottom of the steamer basket, enough to cook the asparagus without touching the water. Bring the water to a simmer, cover the pot, and steam until the stalks are just tender, about 3 minutes. Remove from the steamer and cool the asparagus in the ice-water bath for 1 minute. Drain, then cut into 1-inch pieces and set aside on.

In a 12-inch skillet, heat the olive oil over medium heat. Season the shrimp with salt and pepper, add them to the skillet, and sauté until they just start to turn orange, about 1 minute per side. Using a slotted spoon, transfer the shrimp to a bowl and cover with foil. Add the shallot to the oil that is left in the pan, reduce the heat to low, and cook for about 3 minutes, scraping the browned bits from the bottom of the skillet with a wooden spoon. Add the stock and bring to a boil. Add the coconut milk, bring to a boil again, and boil until the sauce starts to concentrate, thicken, and reduce by half, about 3 minutes.

Reduce the heat to low and add the pasta, shrimp, and asparagus, tossing vigorously to coat everything with the sauce. If needed, add a little pasta cooking water or stock and some coconut milk to keep the dish creamy. Season with salt and pepper and stir in the cognac and chives. Transfer to warm serving bowls and serve immediately.

Escondidinho de Pato com Purê de Aipim
DUCK AND YUCCA SHEPHERD'S PIE

Bazzar, another great restaurant that popped up after I left Rio, opened its doors in 1998. Here I am including my favorite dish on the menu, *escondidinho*, the Brazilian equivalent of shepherd's pie. The name comes from the verb *esconder*, which means "to hide," referring to the meat hidden under a layer of starch. You can make this recipe in stages; if you have the chance to season the duck the night (or up to 3 days) before, great; if not, not a big deal. The entire pie can be assembled ahead and kept in the refrigerator for up to 5 days. This recipe elevates the kitchen skills of the home cook, taking carioca home cooking to a level approaching alchemy.

SERVES 8–10

8 whole duck legs, trimmed of excess fat (½ pound per leg)

Kosher salt and freshly ground black pepper

3 tablespoons olive oil

2 carrots, cut into 1-inch pieces

2 celery stalks, cut into 1-inch pieces

1 large onion, thickly sliced

2 bay leaves

Freshly grated nutmeg

Pinch of paprika

Pinch of cayenne pepper

½ cup dry white wine

4 cups chicken stock

4 bacon slices, diced

4 garlic cloves, minced

1 medium onion, finely diced

1 teaspoon dried oregano

4 plum tomatoes, peeled, seeded, and diced

½ cup chopped fresh parsley

Position an oven rack at the bottom position and preheat to 325°F.

Season the duck with salt and pepper on both sides.

Heat 1 tablespoon of the olive oil in a large Dutch oven over medium-high heat. Working in batches, add the duck legs skin side down and brown them on both sides, about 4 minutes per side (you are looking for gorgeously golden crisp skin). The legs will render a lot of fat; have a small bowl nearby and spoon the fat out. Transfer the duck to a bowl and cover with aluminum foil to keep it moist.

To the fat that's left in the pan (if there is too much, spoon some out), add the carrots, celery, sliced onion, and bay leaves. Season lightly with salt and pepper, nutmeg, and the paprika and cayenne. Reduce the heat to medium-low and cook until the vegetables are softened, stirring often with a wooden spoon, 6 to 8 minutes.

Add the wine and bring to a boil, scraping with a wooden spoon to release the browned bits from the bottom of the pan. Reduce the wine by half, about 3 minutes. Add the stock and bring to a boil. Return the duck to the pan; it should be almost covered in broth (if not, add more stock or water). Cover the pan and transfer to the oven. Cook until the duck is very tender, 1½ to 2 hours, checking often to make sure the liquid is simmering and the liquid level is right—the duck legs should look like alligators at rest in a swamp; if not, add more stock or water.

Remove from the oven and let rest for 30 minutes. (At this point you can cool the dish, transfer the duck and sauce to a storage container with a tight-fitting lid, and refrigerate for up to 3 days.)

When the duck is cool enough to handle, remove it from the cooking liquid. Strain, reserving the broth and discarding the vegetables (hold on to them to add to the filling if you like). Thinly shred the meat (you should have about 5 cups) and set aside. Discard the skin and bones or save it for duck stock.

Preheat the oven to 350°F and grease a 9 x 13-inch baking dish.

Heat the remaining 2 tablespoons olive oil in a large skillet over medium heat. Add the bacon and cook, stirring frequently, until it just begins to get crisp, about 4 minutes. Add the garlic and cook until it just

YUCCA TOPPING

3 pieces yucca (about
2¼ pounds), peeled and
cut into 2-inch pieces

Kosher salt

¾ cup heavy cream

3 tablespoons unsalted butter,
at room temperature

Freshly ground black pepper

8 ounces goat cheese,
crumbled

¼ cup freshly grated Parmesan
cheese

COOKING TIP: My formal
culinary training instinct
tells me never to pass a
tuber vegetable such as
potato—or in this case,
yucca (also known as manioc
or cassava)—through a
food mill. But I noticed
that many Brazilians run
yucca through a blender!
So I decided to give it a try,
and I have to admit that
when working with yucca,
it simply doesn't mash as
easily as potatoes, so even
though it goes against all
instincts, using a blender or
food processor here comes
in handy. (But if this is
still against your cooking
principals, try using an
electric mixer with the
paddle attachment; it's the
middle point between a food
processor and a food mill,
at least regarding yucca.)

begins to turn golden, about 1 minute. Add the diced onion and the oregano, season lightly with salt and pepper, and cook for about 2 minutes, adjusting the heat as necessary. Add the tomatoes and cook until they start to break down and release their liquid, 3 to 4 minutes. Add the shredded duck and stir well. Pour in between 2 and 2½ cups of the reserved broth—you want to have just enough liquid in the pan to moisten the duck. Taste and season with salt and pepper. (If you saved the vegetables from the braising liquid, cut them into small dice and add them now.) Bring to a simmer for 10 minutes for the flavors to meld. Add the parsley, spread the duck into the prepared baking dish, and let cool.

To make the yucca topping, place the yucca in a large saucepan, add water to cover by about 1 inch, add a large pinch of salt, and bring to a boil over high heat. Reduce the heat to low and cook until the yucca is tender enough to be pierced easily with the tip of a knife, 20 to 25 minutes.

Meanwhile, in small saucepan, warm the heavy cream.

Drain the yucca, then place it in the bowl of a food processor. With the machine running, add the hot cream and the butter through the feed tube and process until smooth. Season with salt and pepper.

Spread the yucca over the duck filling, smoothing it evenly with a spatula. Some liquid from the duck might appear—that's okay. Sprinkle with the goat cheese and Parmesan cheese. Place the pie on a baking sheet to catch any dripping juices and bake until hot and bubbly, about 30 minutes.

Let cool for 15 minutes before serving.

RESTAURANT: Bazzar, R. Barão
da Torre, 538 Rio de Janeiro
bazzar.com.br

Pipoca Doce das Esquinas do Rio
SWEET COCOA POPCORN

João Pereira Ramos Neto is proud to say he is a *pipoqueiro,* a person who sells popcorn. He moved from Paraíba, northeast of Brazil, to Rio to seek a better life, and found it with the *jeitinho*: that singularly Brazilian ability to adapt, be clever, and make do with whatever one has. He parks his cart in the corner of Praça Nossa Senhora da Paz in Ipanema and sells popcorn every afternoon. It is fascinating to watch as the line forms and he opens the *saquinho* (little bag) with the scooper. The sound of corn popping is as enticing as the smell, especially for *pipoca doce,* the sweet caramelized version. "Each grain of corn must be coated with a thin caramel, flavored with chocolate, and you can't stop churning the pan," he explains. My love affair with *pipoca doce* dates back to the 1970s when I was a little girl begging my mom, who is also a popcorn addict, for another *saquinho*. To make this recipe, I bought a popcorn popper pan (I got mine at Crate & Barrel) and followed João's advice.

MAKES 6 CUPS, ENOUGH FOR 4 SERVINGS

1 tablespoon Nescau or Nesquik

6 tablespoons sugar

¼ cup vegetable oil

⅓ cup popcorn kernels

INGREDIENT NOTE:
Nescau is a sweetened cocoa powder created by Nestlé for Brazil, and can be found in any Brazilian store or online. You can substitute the US version, Nesquik.

In a large popcorn popper pan, combine the Nescau, sugar, and vegetable oil. Place over medium heat and bring to a boil, stirring frequently with a wooden spoon.

As soon as the mixture starts to bubble, add the popcorn kernels, cover and lock the pan, reduce the heat to low, and cook, turning the handle slowly but constantly all the while. After about 4 minutes, the pan will smoke, and the corn will start popping for the last 2 minutes.

Immediately open the lid and pour the popcorn into a large bowl. Let cool to room temperature and toss, breaking up any clusters of caramel. In dry conditions, the popcorn will stay crunchy stored in a tightly covered container for up to 2 weeks. If humidity causes it to lose its crunch, reheat in a preheated 300°F oven for 10 minutes to bring it back to crunchy.

COPACABANA
& LEME

COPACABANA AND LEME: MUSIC AND FOOD

Another borough, another song. "Copacabana" is the sound of Rio gone global. It's branded. Who can resist dancing to the rhythm and lyrics of the famous Barry Manilow song? Rio's magical places have the power to inspire musicians and artists from around the world. Indeed, music and passion are always in fashion at the *Copa! Copacabana!*

Copacabana is regal, and many world celebrities stay at the majestic Copacabana Palace Hotel, a landmark that adds plenty of history to the borough. Another king of music, Barry White, wrote "Rio de Janeiro," possibly while staying at the famous hotel located in Copacabana.

I've spent many New Year's Eves at the Copacabana, one of the greatest shows on earth. The wide and broad dark yellow sands of the Copacabana and Leme neighborhoods are stage to some of the greatest film, sports, and music festivals in Rio.

Copacabana and Leme are also about secrets, surprises, and supremacy passed down through generations of cariocas, attracting some of the older and wiser age group, as if only they can exercise on the breezy boardwalk before the sun gets too hot and catch a

beautiful whisper of the wind that blows through the bay.

Also bringing a sense of historical style are the galerias, mini plazas uniting commerce at street level with corporate and medical offices cluttered at the entrances. At Galeria Menescal, one of the most traditional plazas in the neighborhood, you can find the most incredible *esfiha de carne* from Baalbeck; see my version on page 57.

This chapter features both traditional carioca recipes and some of my own creations inspired by ingredients I find in Copacabana, like the Choco Nut Cake on page 65. Put on some Brazilian music (among many Brazilian artists, I am addicted to Marisa Monte, my fellow carioca) or Barry Manilow's "Copacabana" and bring a little Rio into your home with these recipes.

Açorda Alantejana
GARLIC AND CILANTRO SOUP WITH POACHED EGGS AND CROUTONS

RESTAURANT: Restaurante Alfaia
R. Inhangá, 30 – Copacabana
restaurantalfaia.com.br

This soup, another dish with a Portuguese influence, is one I can always rely on, as most of the ingredients will already be at hand at my house. I eat this soup at Alfaia, where they make it with water rather than stock, giving the garlic the duty of flavoring the broth, but I find that chicken stock elevates it to a whole new level, making for a rich, full, fragrantly deep soup with a flavor that can only come from a good stock. Then there is the cilantro, which is one of the most commonly used herbs in Brazil. If you're not a fan of cilantro, you can substitute the same amount of parsley leaves or 2 cups shredded collard greens.

SERVES 4

2 cups crustless bread, cut into ½-inch cubes

¼ cup plus 2 tablespoons extra virgin olive oil

Kosher salt and freshly ground black pepper

1 teaspoon white wine vinegar

4 large eggs

3 garlic cloves, finely minced

5 cups chicken stock

5 cups packed fresh cilantro leaves

Preheat the oven to 350°F. Place the bread cubes in a medium bowl and drizzle 2 tablespoons of the olive oil over them. Season with salt and pepper and toss to coat with the oil. Place in the oven and toast, stirring once halfway through, until the bread cubes just begin to get crisp, about 15 minutes. Remove from the oven and set aside.

Fill a bowl with ice and water. Bring a saucepan of water to a simmer over medium heat, add the vinegar, and mix well. Break each egg into a cup or ramekin and gently transfer the eggs from the bowls into the simmering water, coming as close as you can to the water as you add them. Poach the eggs until the whites are set but the yolks remain runny, about 3 minutes. Using a slotted spoon, remove each egg from the simmering water and transfer to the iced water bath for 2 to 3 minutes. Transfer to a plate lined with paper towels and cover loosely with foil.

In a large saucepan, heat the remaining ¼ cup olive oil over low heat. Add the garlic and cook until it just starts to turn golden and become fragrant, about 3 minutes. Slowly stir in the chicken stock and season with salt and pepper.

Add the cilantro leaves just as you are ready to serve. Divide the toasted bread cubes and eggs among the soup bowls, ladle the soup on top, and serve.

Sopa de Castanha do Pará
CREAMY BRAZIL NUT SOUP

STORE: Casas Pedro
R. Barata Ribeiro, 370 –
Copacabana, casaspedro.com.br

The day I went to the specialty store, Casas Pedro, I bought more Brazil nuts than I knew what to do with. I've read all about the health benefits of Brazil nuts, but I adore *castanha do pará* because eating them brings together all the wonderful elements of a nut and a coconut in a single pod. I often use Brazil nuts for baking, but I also love them in this savory soup. The coconutty flavors from the Brazil nut makes this warm and creamy soup a revelation.

SERVES 4

1½ cups Brazil nuts

4 cups chicken stock, hot

Kosher salt and freshly ground black pepper

2 tablespoons butter

1 tablespoons extra virgin olive oil

1 medium onion, chopped

3 garlic cloves

⅛ teaspoon cayenne pepper

½ teaspoon paprika

2 tablespoons all-purpose flour

½ cup heavy cream

Preheat the oven to 325°F. Place the Brazil nuts on a baking sheet, place them in the oven, and roast until they just start to become aromatic, about 12 minutes. Transfer to a plate and cool completely. Rub the Brazil nuts between your hands or use a dishtowel to peel away the thin brown skin; it should come off quite easily.

Place the Brazil nuts in a food processor and process until completely ground. Add a ladle of the hot stock and season with salt and pepper.

In a medium saucepan, melt the butter in the olive oil over low heat. Add the onion and cook, stirring occasionally with a wooden spoon, until softened and translucent, 3 to 5 minutes. Add the garlic and stir, then add the cayenne and paprika. Add the flour and cook, stirring constantly, until the flour just begins to foam, about 2 minutes.

Add the nut mixture and the remaining chicken stock. Season with salt and pepper, bring to a simmer, cover, and simmer for 5 to 10 minutes, until heated through.

Working in batches, puree the soup in a blender. Return the soup to a pot, place over low heat, add the heavy cream, and bring to a simmer again. Taste and adjust the seasonings, then ladle into warmed soup bowls and serve.

Esfiha do Baalbeck
SAVORY MIDDLE EASTERN PASTRIES

Cariocas love street food and that may be one of the reasons why we embrace Mediterranean cuisine so well, especially kibbes and esfihas. At Baalbeck, I don't sit down. There is something about that place that brings my sense of taste to full gear by eating standing up, leaning over the balcony, while talking to my mother and brother about just how delicious everything there tastes. The esfiha at Baalbeck is special; the dough is light, almost crunchy, shaped in a triangle and stuffed with a variety of fillings like ricotta and spinach, chicken, or meat. Here I use a meat filling, but do know that you can use this dough with just about any type of filling.

MAKES ABOUT 35

DOUGH

2¼ teaspoons (1 envelope) active dry yeast

¼ cup warm water

1 teaspoon sugar

⅓ cup extra virgin olive oil, plus more for glazing

¼ cup canola oil

1 cup room-temperature water

4 cups all-purpose flour, sifted

2 teaspoons kosher salt

FILLING

1 pound ground beef

2 garlic cloves, finely minced

1 small red onion, finely diced

2 scallions, green parts only, chopped

Kosher salt and freshly ground black pepper

2 plum tomatoes, seeded and diced

Juice of 1 lime

½ cup pine nuts

1 tablespoon chopped fresh parsley

RESTAURANT: Baalbeck
Av. N. S. de Copacabana, 664, lj 17
(Galeria Menescal)

Prepare the dough: In a small bowl, whisk the yeast with ¼ cup warm water. Add the sugar and whisk until the sugar and yeast are dissolved. Let sit until the mixture begins to bubble, about 10 minutes.

Add the olive oil, canola oil, and the 1 cup room-temperature water to the yeast mixture.

In the bowl of an electric mixer fitted with the hook attachment, combine the flour and salt. Turn the machine to low speed, slowly pour in the yeast mixture, and beat until the dough becomes structured and elastic, about 5 minutes.

Scrape the dough into an oiled bowl. Press a piece of plastic wrap against the dough and let rise until doubled in size, about 30 minutes. (At this point you can store the dough in the refrigerator for up to 2 days; bring to room temperature 30 minutes before using.)

Meanwhile, prepare the filling: Place the beef in a bowl, add the garlic, onion, and scallions, and mix well. Season with salt and pepper. Add the tomatoes and lime juice and mix well. Place the filling inside a colander over a bowl; cover loosely with plastic wrap and let sit for about 30 minutes to drain any juices. Transfer the filling to a bowl and add the pine nuts and parsley. Set aside.

Make the *esfihas*: Scrape the dough out of the bowl onto a floured surface and press into a square about ½ inch thick. Divide the dough into 4 equal pieces. Cover lightly with plastic wrap while you work with one piece at a time. Roll each piece of dough into a log measuring about 10 inches and cut each piece into 8 equal pieces. Turn each piece so that the inside of the log is facing up.

Using a rolling pin, roll each piece of dough into a 3½-inch round (I like to use a 3½-inch round cookie cutter to help keep my circles uniform). Place 1 tablespoon of filling in the middle of each round and brush the edges with water. Fold two sides of the circle toward the middle, then bring in the third side to close it into a triangle. Pinch to secure the edges. Repeat with the remaining dough and filling. Place on 2 baking sheets lined with parchment paper about 1 inch apart and let rise for 30 to 60 minutes, until risen and puffy.

Meanwhile, set 2 racks in the middle positions of the oven and preheat the oven to 350°F.

Brush the esfihas with olive oil and bake, turning once halfway through, until light golden in color, 16 to 18 minutes. Cool for a few minutes on a wire rack and serve warm.

Bilinis de Moqueca de Camarão
MOQUECA BLINIS WITH SHRIMP

RESTAURANT: Le Pré Catalan
v. Atlântica, 4240 – Copacabana
leprecatalan.com.br

The first time I tasted Rolland Villar's cooking, I learned it was foolish to think that only Brazilian chefs can truly understand Brazilian cuisine. Setting base in Rio de Janeiro's Sofitel Hotel, he oversees the cuisine for all Sofitel hotels in South America. Le Pré Catelan, the French-named jewel restaurant of the chain, pays homage to the land that has welcomed Chef Villar with open arms, combining iconic ingredients from Brazilian gastronomy with the sophistication and refinement of French cuisine. Among Villar's many amazing creations are these moqueca blinis. He thickens a classic *moqueca* (fish stew) with a simple flour mixture, then adds baking powder, egg yolks, and whipped egg whites. When it meets the skillet, the flavors of a moqueca in the shape of a blini is an explosion of joy, creativity, and Brazil!

MAKES 35

¾ cup breadcrumbs

¼ cup all-purpose flour

3 tablespoons dendê oil, plus more for drizzling

½ red bell pepper, roughly chopped

½ green bell pepper, roughly chopped

½ yellow bell pepper, roughly chopped

½ medium onion, roughly chopped

2 garlic cloves, minced

1¼ cups coconut milk

1 tablespoon tomato paste

Kosher salt and freshly ground black pepper

Freshly grated nutmeg

Pinch of cayenne pepper

Pinch of paprika, plus more for sprinkling

¼ cup chopped fresh cilantro

4 large eggs, separated

1½ teaspoons baking powder

2 tablespoons unsalted butter

1 pound fresh small shrimp, peeled and deveined

2 tablespoons olive oil

In a medium bowl, whisk the breadcrumbs with the flour. Set aside.

In a large skillet, heat the dendê oil over medium heat. Add the bell peppers and onion and cook, stirring frequently with a wooden spoon, until softened, 5 to 8 minutes. Add the garlic and cook for another 2 minutes. Add the coconut milk and tomato paste, reduce the heat to low, and cook until the mixture starts to thicken, about 5 minutes. Season with salt, pepper, nutmeg, the cayenne, and paprika. Add the cilantro and breadcrumb mixture and stir well with a wooden spoon.

Transfer the mixture to a food processor and process until completely smooth, about 3 minutes. At this point the mixture will become a paste.

Scrape the mixture into a large bowl and add the egg yolks, one at a time, mixing well with a rubber spatula after each addition. Add the baking powder and mix well.

In the bowl of an electric mixer fitted with the whisk attachment, beat the egg whites until soft peaks form, about 5 minutes. Using a rubber spatula, carefully fold the whites into the moqueca mixture. The batter can be frozen in an airtight container for up to 3 months.

Heat a large nonstick skillet or grill pan over medium heat. Drop a pinch of butter the size of a pea into the pan and swirl it around. Pour 2 to 3 tablespoons of batter onto the skillet and cook until golden brown on the bottom and tiny holes appear on the surface, about 2 minutes. Turn the blini over and cook until golden on the other side, about another minute. Transfer to a plate and repeat making blinis with the remaining batter. (You can prepare the blinis ahead of time; keep them stacked and wrapped in foil in the refrigerator for up to 5 days. To reheat, remove the foil and place the stack in a preheated 350°F oven and heat for 5 minutes.)

Season the shrimp with salt and pepper on both sides. Heat the olive oil in a medium skillet over medium heat. Add the shrimp and cook just until they turn orange, about 1 minute per side.

Stack 3 blinis on each plate and top with 3 shrimp. Sprinkle with paprika and a drizzle of dendê oil.

Torta de Espinafre
CREAMY CHEESY SPINACH PIE

RESTAURANT: The Bakers
Rua Santa Clara, 86 – Copacabana
thebakers.com.br

Just a few steps from Avenida Nossa Senhora de Copacabana, the smell of cakes, tarts, and *folheados* travels a far distance, even among all the cabs, buses, and cars that crowd the section of Rio that houses The Bakers. In this recipe, I departed from the original dough used in *empadão* (a savory baked double-crusted pie; our version of quiche) by making the whole crust in the food processor using salty crackers. The filling is classic. The Bakers have a spinach *folheado* that is killer, creamy and cheesy at the center, and I've reproduced that here.

SERVES 4–6

CRUST

62 Ritz crackers

5 tablespoons unsalted butter, melted and cooled

FILLING

1 pound frozen spinach, thawed

2 strips bacon, cut into strips

2 tablespoons extra virgin olive oil

2 shallots, finely chopped

2 cups whole milk

6 tablespoons butter, plus more for the ramekins

6 tablespoons all-purpose flour

Kosher salt and freshly ground pepper

Freshly grated nutmeg

Cayenne pepper

½ cup grated Gruyere cheese

¼ cup grated Parmesan cheese

Preheat the oven to 350°F.

To make the crust, place the crackers in a food processor and grind until evenly crumbled. With the motor still running, slowly drizzle in the butter through the feed tube until the crumbs are uniformly moist. Using your hands, press the mixture into a 9-inch round baking pan, patting an even layer on the bottom and all the way up the sides. Bake for 12 to 14 minutes, then cool on a wire rack.

Put the spinach in a sieve and press out as much liquid as possible, then roughly chop it.

In a medium skillet, heat the bacon in the olive oil over medium heat until slightly crisp, about 3 minutes. Add the shallots and cook, stirring occasionally, until softened and translucent, about 3 minutes. Add the spinach and mix until well combined. Remove from the heat.

In a small saucepan, bring the milk to a simmer.

In a medium saucepan, melt the butter over low heat. Add the flour, mix well with a wooden spoon, and cook until it starts to foam, about 2 minutes.

In one stroke, add the milk to the butter-flour mixture and cook, whisking constantly, until smooth, about 3 minutes. Season with salt, pepper, nutmeg, and cayenne.

Off the heat, mix the milk into the spinach mixture; taste to make sure it's well seasoned. Add the Gruyère cheese. Pour the filling into the cooled crust and spread evenly with a spatula. Sprinkle the Parmesan cheese on top. (This can be done up to 2 days ahead of time; cover with plastic wrap and refrigerate.)

Place in the oven and bake until golden and set, about 30 minutes. Cool on a wire rack for 15 minutes, then serve with a salad.

Bem Casado
BRAZILIAN SANDWICH COOKIE

Elvira Bona is a Maranhense (a person born in the state of Maranhão) who now lives in Rio de Janeiro, where she bakes up to five thousand *bem casados* a week from her kitchen in Copacabana and ships them throughout the country.

The literal translation for *bem casado* is "well married," meaning that one cookie should be perfectly fitted with the other. They can be filled with dulce de leche, lemon cream, passion fruit curd, *ovos moles* (see page 107), chocolate ganache, or apricot jam.

Cariocas go wild about the presentation of *bem casado,* and according to Elvira, dressing up the treat requires more work than the preparation itself. The presentation follows the theme of the occasion, from the birth of a baby to weddings and other parties. If you want to dress up your *bem casado*, you may want to visit your favorite craft store for inspiration.

MAKES ABOUT 25

3 large eggs

3 large egg yolks

Pinch of salt

½ cup sugar

½ cup cake flour

¼ cup cornstarch

SUGAR GLAZE

2 cups confectioners' sugar

⅓ cup warm water

½ teaspoon vanilla extract

INGREDIENT NOTE:
For jam or dulce de leche, buy a high-quality brand like La Salamandra. For chocolate ganache, bring 1 cup heavy cream to a simmer, turn off the heat, and add 8 ounces chopped bittersweet chocolate; whisk in 4 tablespoons butter and cool.

Preheat the oven to 350°F. Line 2 baking sheets with parchment paper.

Fill a pot large enough to hold the bowl of an electric mixer with a few inches of water and bring to a simmer.

In the bowl of an electric mixer, whisk the eggs, egg yolks, salt, and sugar to combine. Place the bowl over the simmering water without touching the water and whisk constantly until the mixture is lukewarm, about 2 minutes. Transfer the bowl to the mixer fitted with the whisk attachment and beat on high speed until the egg mixture is pale, thick, and has tripled in volume, about 10 minutes.

While the machine is running, sift the flour and cornstarch into a medium bowl. Once your 10 minutes mixing time is up, sprinkle one third of the flour over the eggs. Fold with a rubber spatula, reaching to the bottom of the bowl in every pass to prevent lumps from forming. Repeat with another third of the flour mixture, and then the final third.

Fit a pastry bag with a plain round number 6 tip. Pour half of the batter inside and pipe 2-inch circles about 1 inch apart on the prepared baking sheets. Repeat with the second half of batter.

Bake until golden brown, 8 to 10 minutes (any longer and the cookies will get too crunchy). Let cool on the baking sheets.

Lay the cookies on a work surface. Elvira likes to scrape the middle of each cookie lightly with a teaspoon (to create even more room for filling), but make your own call. Fill the cookies with about 1 tablespoon of the filling of your choice (I like to use a pastry bag for this task) and sandwich them closed.

Make the sugar glaze: Sift the confectioners' sugar into a bowl. Pour in the warm water and whisk well, making sure there are no lumps of sugar. If it's too thin, you can always add more sugar. Whisk in the vanilla.

Using a chocolate fork, drop each *bem casado* into the sugar glaze until it's just coated, then transfer to a wire rack set over a baking sheet. Allow to dry completely, about 1 hour. Be careful when removing the cookie from the rack as the glaze tends to get caught on the bottom. Store in an airtight container in a dry place for up to 3 days. For a carioca-style party presentation, wrap each *bem casado* individually in cellophane and crepe paper and tie it with a beautiful ribbon.

Pão de Mel
CHOCOLATE-COVERED HONEY BREADS WITH DULCE DE LECHE FILLING

If you grew up in Rio, then you certainly know the chocolate store Kopenhagen. You may also know *lingua de gato*, a milk chocolate in the shape of a cat's tongue. How about *nha benta* (see page 176)? Another favorite of mine is *pão de mel*, wrapped individually for each solo indulgence. Many people swear that this tastes like honey, and while honey is a powerful ingredient in the recipe, the reason I love *pão de mel* is for the bigger picture: contrary to what the name indicates (*pão* means bread), there is nothing bready about this treat, a dark and decadent sandwich honey cake filled with dulce de leche and encased in chocolate.

MAKES ABOUT 20

2¼ cups all-purpose flour

¼ cup unsweetened cocoa powder

1 teaspoon baking soda

½ teaspoon baking powder

¼ teaspoon salt

1 teaspoon ground cinnamon

¼ teaspoon freshly grated nutmeg

¼ cup ground walnuts

½ cup honey

2 large eggs

2 tablespoons sugar

1 teaspoon vanilla extract

¾ cup vegetable oil

½ cup sweetened condensed milk

1 cup whole milk

1 cup dulce de leche

2 pounds semisweet baking chocolate, chopped

Position a rack in the center of the oven and preheat the oven to 350°F. Coat a 9 x 13-inch baking pan with cooking spray, line the bottom with parchment paper, and spray again.

Sift the flour, cocoa powder, baking soda, baking powder, salt, cinnamon, and nutmeg into a large bowl. Add the ground walnuts and whisk until well combined.

In another large bowl, whisk together the honey, eggs, sugar, vanilla, vegetable oil, condensed milk, and whole milk.

Pour the liquid ingredients over the flour mixture and fold with a rubber spatula to form a batter, making sure there are no pockets of flour remaining. Pour the batter into the prepared pan and smooth the top with a spatula. Bake the cake until the top starts to crack and a toothpick inserted in the middle comes out clean, 35 to 40 minutes.

Transfer the cake to a wire rack and let cool for 10 minutes. Run a knife around the edges, place another rack on top, and flip. Peel the parchment paper off and flip once more so that the cake rests right side up. Cool completely. (The cake can be wrapped in plastic and kept in the refrigerator for up to 5 days in advance.)

Using a long serrated knife, trim the sides and top of the cake. Slice the cake horizontally in half. I like to slice each half once more, for 4 layers total. Using a 2¼-inch round cookie cutter, cut out as many circles as you can from each slice of cake. Discard all the scraps, or make a preview of the finished dessert by spreading some dulce de leche on a piece of scrap and nibbling at it. Transfer the circles of *pão de mel* to a baking sheet and arrange them in pairs, leaving a little space between them. You should have about 40 circles.

Place 1 to 2 tablespoons of dulce de leche between 2 cake circles to make a sandwich, pressing down lightly so that the dulce de leche reaches the edges. Repeat until you have sandwiched all the circles.

Place the chopped chocolate in a heatproof bowl set over of a pan filled with simmering water (not touching the water) and heat the

RESTAURANT: Kopenhagan
Rua Ataulfo de Paiva, 1025 –
Leblon kopenhagen.com.br

COOKING TIP: I prefer not to use hard chocolate in this recipe, as the cake is too big to manage it (while a bonbon would be just perfect). Instead I use dipping chocolate, which doesn't require tempering at all. The truth is that dipping chocolate is not pure chocolate; it is mixed with vegetable fat. In the past, many pastry chefs looked at dipping chocolate with disdain, but in recent years chocolate brands have improved to the point that if you use a high-quality brand no one will ever know it is not pure chocolate. I use Felchlin brand, which comes in pistoles (coin-shaped pieces of chocolate), so you don't even need to chop it. Most often I use store-bought dulce de leche, but you can make your own by cooking a can of sweetened condensed milk in a large pot at a simmer for 4 hours or in a pressure cooker for 1 hour.

chocolate, stirring, until it's just melted. Remove the chocolate from the heat and drop a *pão de mel* into the chocolate glaze and flip to cover the entire outside. Using a chocolate fork, lift it and allow the excess glaze to drop. Place on a baking sheet covered with parchment paper. Repeat until all the *pão de mel* are covered.

Bolo de Chocolate com Castanha do Pará e Côco

CHOCOLATE, BRAZIL NUT, AND COCONUT CAKE

One sunny summer day in Rio, I was visiting Casas Pedro, a store in Copacabana (see box on page 56), where you can easily spend an hour browsing through nuts, spices, and condiments. I fell into a chat with the vendor, who told me that a bag of *castanha do pará* (Brazil nuts) had just arrived. By the end of my shopping spree, I'd gotten a handful of nuts, coconut, and a few other Brazilian ingredients. I knew exactly what I wanted to prepare with these treasures: a Brazil nut cake, one that features chocolate prominently. All those nuts were screaming for chocolate, and so was I! This chewy chocolate torte, nicknamed Choco Nut Cake, packs more Brazilian flavor than most chocolate desserts, making it very gratifying to make. One word of caution: it is very important to keep the cake moist; so, just as you would do for a brownie, take care not to overbake it.

SERVES 6–8

6 ounces semisweet chocolate, chopped

1¼ cups Brazil nuts

1¼ cups unsweetened grated coconut

½ cup (1 stick) unsalted butter, at room temperature

⅔ cup sugar

4 large eggs

1 teaspoon coconut extract or rum

Cocoa powder for garnish

Preheat the oven to 350°F. Butter a 9-inch round cake pan, line the bottom with parchment paper, butter again and dust with flour.

Place the chocolate in a heatproof bowl set over of a pan filled with simmering water (not touching the water). Heat until melted, then remove from the heat.

In a food processor, process the Brazil nuts and coconut until finely ground, about 30 seconds. (All nuts release oil when ground, and Brazil nuts contain lots of oil, so be careful not to let the mixture turn into a paste.) Transfer to a bowl.

Using the same food processor bowl, process the butter and sugar until smooth.

With the motor running, add the eggs, one at a time, and the coconut extract or rum and process until smooth, stopping occasionally to scrape the sides of the bowl.

Add the nut mixture and melted chocolate and pulse to blend. Pour the batter into the prepared cake pan and spread evenly with a spatula.

Bake until the center is slightly puffed, 25 to 28 minutes. Transfer to a wire rack to cool for 15 minutes, then invert onto a serving plate, peel the parchment paper off, and invert again. Cool completely. Sprinkle cocoa powder all over the cake just before serving.

JARDIM BÔTANICO, GÁVEA & LAGOA

JARDIM BOTÂNICO, GÁVEA, & LAGOA: TROPICAL WONDERS

My mid-1970s childhood in Rio was a tropical wonderland of *pedalinho na lagoa* (pedaling in a swan boat on the lagoon), going to Clube Caiçaras (a club that was practically my second home in Rio), also located at Lagoa, and many walking tours through the Jardim Botânico (Rio's botanical garden).

I was comforted by *empadinhas* from Chez Anne (page 72) and often craved fruit ice cream from Mil Frutas (page 81), places I visit often every time I go back. Lunch at Caicaras was often steak with mustard sauce (page 73) while watching handsome men row on Lagoa Rodrigo de Freitas. It's impossible to live in Rio without looking at its beautiful people, without feeling the joy of being alive, without singing the lyrics of the music, without feeling the heat oozing through your pores. In Rio, life is a party, every day of the year.

Cariocas are obsessed with exercise, and Lagoa Rodrigo de Freitas (a lagoon) is one of the most beautiful places in town to go jogging. Although the reasons behind exercising are usually straightforward and rational—we exercise because we want to stay healthy or lose weight—exercising in Rio becomes more than just that: it's as if your endorphins double from the visual effects of Rio, and the result is a sense of pure happiness, elation, and peacefulness. There is even a local slang word for exercising in Rio, called *malhar*.

Jardim Botânico was created by King Dom João VI of Portugal in 1808, initially to grow herbs and spices brought from India. Each time I visit Jardim Botânico, something different captures my attention. The trees are so huge you wonder how many years ago they were planted. One of the main species of trees there is the pau Brazil, which is a huge part of the history of Brazil. It was found all over the coast when the country was first colonized and it is where Brazil got its name. The tall palm trees, also known as Imperial palms, were planted by Dom João in 1809 and today are the main symbol of the garden. Native to Central America and Guyana, these palm trees can reach up to 150 feet in height.

Along my way to adulthood, a certain muted luxury became the hallmark of Jardim Botânico, with more established urban chefs setting down roots. Years ago Chef Claude Troisgros opened a restaurant there, now named Olympe, in honor of his mother. His bass with caramelized bananas (page 78) is the kind of recipe that will impress your guests with zero effort. You also get a sense of this untamed extravaganza at places like Bráz Pizzaria, where cariocas mingle outside the restaurant, particularly on Sunday nights. I love their sausage bread and have included my version in this chapter.

This section of Rio is very close to my childhood home, and choosing which recipes to feature was quite a challenge. The following recipes are just a sampling of the riches from this beloved neighborhood of Rio.

Pão de Calabresa da Pizzaria Braz
ROLLED SAUSAGE BREAD WITH ROSEMARY

RESTAURANT: Bráz Pizzaria, R. Maria Angélica, 129 – Jardim Botânico, brazpizzaria.com.br

It wasn't until I left Rio that Bráz Pizzaria came from São Paulo to Jardim Botânico. Now every time I travel home, I run to Bráz Pizzaria to devour *pão de calabresa*, a generous, well-burnished round bread baked inside a tube mold. Even though this may be a classic in Italy, in Rio it is still a novelty. The appeal of this bread is not a mystery to cariocas: we love *linguiça calabresa* any way we can get it—and this bread is all about the sausage. Make sure to use a high-quality brand that you love.

I took a cue for the dough for this bread from my friend Nick Malgieri, and this bread is the absolute best food for sharing with a large crowd. Okay, so you're going to be full before you start eating—who cares? And if you have the chance to visit Bráz Pizzaria, I suggest you order the sausage bread as well as a bunch of different pizzas, because every pizza there is wonderful, especially the ones with Catupiry cream cheese.

SERVES 16

4 cups all-purpose flour

2½ teaspoons salt

2 teaspoons (1 envelope) dry yeast

1⅔ cups warm water

5 tablespoons olive oil

1 pound linguica, cut into ¼-inch-thick slices

Leaves of 3 sprigs of fresh rosemary, roughly chopped

Sift the flour and salt in a large bowl.

In a small bowl, whisk the yeast into the water and let sit for about 5 minutes, until bubbling. Whisk in 3 tablespoons of the olive oil.

Using a rubber spatula, make a well in the center of the flour. Pour in the yeast mixture and, using the spatula, stir in a circular motion, incorporating more flour as you stir. Drop the spatula and use your hands to knead the dough, making sure there are no dry bits of flour at the bottom of the bowl and the dough is smooth. Transfer the dough to a clean large bowl greased with oil. Cover with lightly oiled plastic wrap and let rest in a warm spot until it doubles in size, 1 to 2 hours, depending on the temperature of the room.

Meanwhile, heat the remaining 2 tablespoons olive oil in a large skillet over medium heat. Add the sausage and cook, stirring frequently, until crisp, 8 to 10 minutes. Drain the sausage in a plate covered with paper towels and let cool completely.

Invert the dough onto a floured surface and press it down to deflate. Divide the dough into 3 equal pieces. Working with one piece at a time, roll the dough out into a slightly rounded rectangular shape of about 14 x 8 inches, distribute a third of the sausage over it, and sprinkle with a few rosemary leaves. Starting at the far end of the dough, roll it toward you, jelly-roll style, pinching the edges when you get to the end. Roll out the second piece of dough and spread a second third of the sausage all over, followed by some rosemary leaves. Now, before you continue, place the first rolled piece of dough on top of the second piece of dough, toward the start, and roll it up around the first piece. Repeat with the third piece, placing the previous 2 rolls inside. By the time the 3 pieces of dough are stuffed and rolled, you will have a jelly-roll shape of about 3½ inches in diameter. Trim both ends.

Grease an 8-cup tube pan with vegetable oil. Fit the dough inside the prepared pan seam side up. (If the length of the dough is longer than that of the mold, you can overlap. If it's shorter, bring the dough back to the work surface and stretch it.) Cover with oiled plastic wrap and let rise

until doubled in size, 1 to 2 hours (or refrigerate overnight). When risen, the dough will be about 1 inch above the rim of the pan.

When the dough is almost risen, preheat the oven to 425°F and set a rack in the lower third of the oven.

Bake until the bread is well risen, golden, and firm and the internal temperature is about 200°F, about 30 minutes. Transfer the pan onto a wire rack and let it cool in the pan for about 10 minutes before unmolding. Use a serrated knife to cut it into thick slices.

INGREDIENT NOTE: Brazilian linguiça lends itself to slicing better than breaking, but other sausages might work better crumbled. Know your sausage and use your judgment.

Empadinhas de Queijo do Chez Anne
CHEZ ANNE'S CHEESE EMPANADAS

RESTAURANT: Chez Anne
R. Marquês de São Vicente, 52 –
Gávea chezanne.com.br

Have you ever noticed how few savory snacks are offered in cafés in the United States? In Rio and throughout Brazil, we love savory snacks, and *empadinhas de queijo* are among my favorites. You will find them in almost every corner of the city, and here I'm sharing an easy version to make at home, inspired by Chez Anne, a famous bakery in Rio. Many empanadas are double-crusted, but this one is single-crusted, making it even easier to prepare, and they reheat quite well, making them a great take-away snack.

MAKES 36

DOUGH

3⅓ cups all-purpose flour, sifted

2 teaspoons salt

1½ cups (2½ sticks) chilled unsalted butter, cut into cubes

2 large egg yolks

3 to 4 tablespoons cold water

FILLING

1 pound cottage cheese, drained in a colander overnight

1 tablespoon extra virgin olive oil

1 teaspoon dried oregano

Kosher salt and freshly ground black pepper

½ cup whole milk

½ cup heavy cream

1 large egg

3 tablespoons all-purpose flour

¼ cup tightly packed freshly grated Parmesan cheese

Freshly grated nutmeg

Pinch of cayenne pepper

Make the dough: Place the flour and salt in the bowl of a food processor. Add the butter and pulse about 20 times to mix it in. Add the egg yolks and pulse again to combine. Add the water and pulse until the dough just starts to come together. Place the dough onto a floured surface and gather it into a ball, then shape it into a flat disk. Wrap in plastic wrap and refrigerate for at least 30 minutes. (This can be done up to 2 days ahead.)

Remove the dough from the refrigerator at least 20 minutes before rolling so that it becomes malleable. On a lightly floured surface, roll out the dough ¼ inch thick, and use a round cutter slightly larger than the tartlet molds to cut out dough circles. Cut them close together to get as many rounds as possible. Carefully lift each circle and fit the dough into the bottom and up the sides of each mold, leaving extra dough above the edges. If the dough cracks or splits as you work, patch the cracks with dough scraps using a wet finger to "glue" them in place. Place the molds on a baking sheet and refrigerate while you prepare the filling.

Preheat the oven to 350°F.

In a medium bowl, combine the cottage cheese, olive oil, and oregano and season with salt and pepper. Set aside.

In a blender, combine the milk, cream, egg, flour, and Parmesan cheese and season with salt, pepper, nutmeg, and cayenne. Blend until smooth.

Remove the molds from the refrigerator. Spoon about 1 teaspoon of the cottage cheese mixture into each mold, then carefully pour the liquid mixture on top to within about ¼ inch of the top. Bake until golden brown, about 25 minutes, rotating the molds at least once. Remove from the oven and cool on a wire rack for 5 to 10 minutes before serving.

INGREDIENT NOTE: In Rio we use the most common Brazilian cheese, Minas cheese, see Glossary, page 196. Seeking to make this recipe with ingredients available in the United States, I substituted cottage cheese drained overnight in the refrigerator for the Minas cheese, and it works perfectly. You can also use ricotta if you like.

Bife com Molho de Mostarda e Cebola

STEAK WITH MUSTARD ONION SAUCE

RESTAURANT: Clube Caiçaras, Av. Epitácio Pessoa, s/n – Lagoa, caicaras.com.br

My brother Jimmy's favorite dish growing up was *bife com molho de mostarda* (beef with mustard sauce), which he'd order at Clube Caiçaras, located in Lagoa, a treasured neighborhood in Rio. We still visit the club frequently, and now both my kids and I order this dish, which is still served the same way, the sauce drizzled on top of thin slices of steak. While the sauce can be served with a variety of proteins, it will really shine when paired with a good-quality, tender meat, one that oozes beef juices when cut to the center. You can make this recipe using just one of the two mustards, but I like the flavor nuances the combination of coarse and smooth Dijon mustards contributes to the finished dish.

SERVES 4

1½ pounds beef skirt steak, cut into 4 pieces

Kosher salt and freshly ground black pepper

2 tablespoon unsalted butter, plus more if needed

2 medium onions, thinly sliced

3 tablespoons smooth Dijon mustard

2 tablespoons coarse Dijon mustard

½ cup beef stock or water

½ cup heavy cream

2 tablespoons chopped fresh parsley

Season the meat with salt and pepper on both sides, cover, and refrigerate for at least 2 hours or, preferably, overnight. Let it come to room temperature at least 30 minutes before cooking.

Heat a large heavy skillet over medium-high heat, add the butter, and swirl the pan around. Sear the steaks on both sides until nice and crusty, lowering the heat as needed, cooking until they are done to your liking, 2 to 3 minutes per side for medium-rare. Transfer to a plate and cover tightly with aluminum foil.

Add the onions to the pan and reduce the heat to low. Cook, scraping the browned bits from the skillet with a wooden spoon and adding more butter if necessary, until the onions are softened and browned from the meat juices, about 5 minutes.

Add the mustards and stir well. Add the stock, increase the heat to medium, and bring to a boil. Reduce the heat to low and add the heavy cream; bring to a simmer (don't let it boil or the cream will curdle) and simmer until the sauce is thickened and light brown in color, 2 to 3 minutes.

Return the meat to the pan and warm it for 2 to 3 minutes. Divide the meat among warmed plates, spoon the sauce on top, and garnish with the parsley.

INGREDIENT NOTE: In Brazil, when you say beef (in Portuguese *bife*), we refer to a piece of cow's meat sliced and pounded thin, usually cut from the rump or chuck, rather than cow's meat in general. I suggest skirt steak, or you can try flank steak or filet mignon. I like to sear the meat because it creates that gorgeous brown crust with deep flavors, but you can also grill or roast the meat.

Filet Osvaldo Aranha
STEAK WITH FRIED GARLIC

Filet Osvaldo Aranha is a typical dish served in botequims in Rio de Janeiro, named after Osvaldo Aranha (1894–1960), an important politician who accomplished many noble things in his career but is most remembered for this dish and for being a self-declared foodie. This dish is classically served with rice, potatoes, and toasted manioc starch, but here I stick to the most exciting part of the dish: the steak with fried garlic. You can use other cuts of beef as well, such as hanger, flank, or skirt steak.

SERVES 4

6 garlic cloves

Kosher salt and freshly ground black pepper

Four 4-ounce filet mignons

2 tablespoons canola oil

4 tablespoons unsalted butter

1 tablespoon chopped fresh parsley

Peel and crush the garlic with the side of a chef's knife. Sprinkle with a little salt and finely mince it. You should have about 2 tablespoons minced garlic.

Season the beef with salt and pepper on both sides. Heat a large heavy skillet over medium-high heat, add the oil, and swirl the pan around. Sear the steaks on all sides until nice and crusty, lowering the heat as needed, cooking until they are done to your liking, 2 to 3 minutes per side for medium-rare.

Meanwhile, in a medium skillet, melt the butter over low heat. Add the garlic and cook until light golden brown, swirling the pan frequently to ensure even browning, about 4 minutes.

When the steaks are cooked, place each on a serving plate, spoon the garlic butter on top, and sprinkle with the parsley. Serve immediately.

Stroganoff de Vitela
BRAZILIAN-STYLE VEAL STROGANOFF

RESTAURANT: Braseiro da Gávea
Praça Santos Dumont, 116 – Gávea
casadagavea.org.br

When I was a teenager living in Rio, one of my favorite places to go on a Monday night was Braseiro da Gávea, in Baixo Gávea, where artists, writers, musicians, and just about anybody with an inclination for the bohemian life wandered around. There was a certain *je ne sais quoi* about that night of the week at Braseiro that seemed to draw in the most spectacularly good-looking people in Rio. It was cramped and loud, but that was part of the magic. But that was then; now I like to go to Braseiro—on any given day—for culinary reasons, for example for their Stroganoff.

Beef Stroganoff is one of Russia's greatest dishes; it was named in honor of a member of the Stroganoff family in Russia in the nineteenth century and became popular around the world with many variations. In Brazil you will find differences in the way the recipe is prepared, but also in the protein used: beef, veal, and chicken are the most common. I love veal for its soft slices of tenderloin, but you can also use beef (like Braseiro does) or chicken. My version is not based on a single recipe, but rather a combination of Stroganoffs I've eaten in Rio, and is finished with a mustard-spiked cream sauce. Serve with rice.

SERVES 4

1¼ pounds veal shoulder, cut into 2- to 3-inch-long strips

1 garlic clove, grated

Salt and freshly ground black pepper

5 tablespoons olive oil

1 small onion, chopped

3 garlic cloves, chopped

1 tablespoon Dijon mustard

1 tablespoon all-purpose flour

¼ cup white wine

1¾ cups chicken stock

Freshly grated nutmeg

1¼ cups heavy cream

2 tablespoons chopped fresh parsley

Place the meat in a medium bowl, add the grated garlic, season with salt and pepper, and toss. Cover with plastic wrap and let it sit at room temperature for 1 hour (or refrigerate overnight; if refrigerating, bring to room temperature before cooking).

In a medium Dutch oven, heat 3 tablespoons of the olive oil over medium-high heat and sear the veal (in batches if necessary) until browned on all sides, about 5 minutes. Transfer the meat to a bowl and cover tightly with aluminum foil.

Add the remaining 2 tablespoons olive oil and the onion to the Dutch oven, reduce the heat to low, and cook for about 3 minutes, scraping any browned bits at the bottom of the pan. Add the chopped garlic and cook, stirring, until softened, about 1 minute, and the onion and garlic mixture is dark brown in color. Add the mustard and flour and stir well with a wooden spoon.

Pour in the wine, increase the heat to medium, and cook until most of the wine is absorbed. Add the stock and bring to a boil. Return the meat to the pan, lower the heat, season lightly with salt, pepper, and nutmeg, cover, and simmer gently until the meat is very tender, 40 to 60 minutes. Add more stock if necessary—you want to keep it moist.

Uncover the pan and add the heavy cream. Cook over low heat (don't let it boil or the cream will curdle) until the sauce is thickened and lightly browned, about 10 minutes. Adjust the seasonings and garnish with the parsley.

Quibe de Forno Recheado
BAKED MEAT AND BULGUR PIE

RESTAURANT: Árabe da Gávea
R. Marquês de São Vicente,
52 – Gávea

The influence of Middle Eastern cuisine can be found all over the southeast of Brazil, but my personal attachment to this wonderful cuisine came through my dear friend Tatiana El-Mann, a carioca whose parents emigrated from Lebanon. Tatiana's family cherished the cooking of their birthplace just as much as the language. The conversation in her house was based on the Portuguese language, but animated with tons of Arabic words for which there was simply no translation. Tatiana's mother frequently ordered Middle Eastern foods from Árabe da Gávea, a restaurant located at Shopping da Gávea that specialized in foods from that region. Today I prepare this dish—a Middle Eastern version of meatloaf—in my kitchen as often as I would eat it in Tatiana's house.

SERVE 6–8

1¼ cups fine bulgur

1 cup water

1 medium onion, quartered

1 pound lean ground beef

Kosher salt and freshly
   ground black pepper

Pinch of ground cinnamon

Pinch of freshly grated
   nutmeg

5 tablespoons olive oil

2 tablespoons cold water

MEAT FILLING

3 tablespoons olive oil

1 large onion, finely
   chopped

1½ pounds ground beef,
   veal, or lamb

Kosher salt and freshly
   ground black pepper

Pinch of ground cinnamon

¾ cup pine nuts, slightly
   toasted

Place the bulgur in a fine strainer and rinse with warm water to remove any dirt and excess starch. Drain and place in a large bowl. In a small saucepan, bring the water to a boil and pour it over the bulgur. Cover with aluminum foil and soak until tripled in size, 45 minutes to 1 hour.

Meanwhile, make the meat filling: In a large sauté pan, heat the olive oil over medium heat. Add the chopped onion and cook until softened, 3 to 4 minutes. Add the ground beef and cook, stirring with a wooden spoon, until cooked through and a little crisp, 5 to 8 minutes. Season with salt, pepper, and the cinnamon and stir in the pine nuts. Transfer to a bowl and let cool to room temperature.

Finish the bulgur filling: Place the quartered onion in the bowl of a food processor and process until just chopped. Add the ground beef, season with salt and pepper, and add the cinnamon and nutmeg. Add the soaked bulgur. With the machine running, add 2 tablespoons of the olive oil and the cold water through the feed tube and process until the meat forms into a smooth paste.

Preheat the oven to 375°F. Grease an 8 x 11-inch baking dish with cooking spray.

Using an offset spatula, spread half of the meat paste on the bottom of the baking dish about ¼ inch thick. Spread the meat filling evenly on top and press it down. Now, if you try to spread the remaining paste on top of the meat in one shot with a spatula, the two meats will mix and turn into a big mess. Instead, take small patches of the remaining paste and press it out with the palms of your hands and layer them piece by piece to cover the entire pie.

Using the tip of a paring knife, cut diagonal lines to mark diamond shapes on top of the pie. Brush the remaining 3 tablespoons olive oil over the top and bake until the top is crisp and golden brown, about 40 minutes. Let cool for 5 minutes before serving.

COOKING TIP: I like to serve this with a mint and yogurt sauce: In a bowl, whisk ½ cup plain yogurt, ½ cup sour cream, 1 tablespoon mustard, and a few drops of lime juice. Add 1 tablespoon finely minced red onion and ¼ cup chopped fresh mint and season with salt and pepper. A side of tomatoes and cucumbers works nicely as well.

Filet de Cherne com Banana Caramelada
e Molho Agridoce de Passas

WILD STRIPED BASS WITH CARAMELIZED BANANAS AND GOLDEN RAISIN SAUCE

You've probably heard the term nouvelle cuisine before. Now imagine Brazilian nouvelle cuisine. If you can't, then you must visit Olympe, the restaurant whose chef started it all. Claude Troisgros, son of the legendary chef Jean Pierre Troisgros, landed in Brazil in 1978 after Paul Bocuse asked him if he wanted to spend two years there. Add thirty years and he is still in Rio. I can't help but think that part of what enables Claude to surprise is that he remains, despite all these years, an immigrant in Rio. With a charming heavily accented Portuguese (which has become his trademark) and his deep knowledge of native Brazilian ingredients, he has changed the culinary culture not only of a city, but of a country, inspiring native Brazilian chefs to appreciate their local ingredients. In this dish, one of my favorites of Claude's recipes, the sweetness of the bananas contrasts with the flakiness of the fish, and the rich yet citric sauce is brilliant, typical of Claude. You can also make this recipe with grouper or halibut, or even a thick tilapia fillet.

SERVES 4

GOLDEN RAISIN SAUCE

¾ cup (1½ sticks) unsalted butter

3 tablespoons fresh lemon juice

2 tablespoons soy sauce

1 large shallot, finely minced

1 garlic clove, finely minced

¾ cup golden raisins

3 tablespoons chopped fresh cilantro

4 firm but not green bananas

2 tablespoons unsalted butter

4 pieces skin-on pieces wild striped bass, cut from the thick center portion

Kosher salt and freshly ground pepper

3 tablespoons extra virgin olive oil

Microgreens for garnish (optional)

First make the golden raisin sauce: In a medium saucepan, melt the butter over low heat and cook until it develops a light golden brown color and a nutty aroma, about 4 minutes. Carefully add the lemon juice, soy sauce, shallot, and garlic—it will bubble. Cook, whisking gently, for just 1 minute. Add the golden raisins and swirl the pan around. Remove the pan from the heat and set aside.

Peel and cut the bananas in half lengthwise. Melt the butter in a large nonstick pan over medium heat. Add the bananas, flat side down, and cook until lightly caramelized on both sides, about 2 minutes per side. Remove from the heat and set aside.

Make 2 or 3 small diagonal cuts on the skin of the fish without piercing the flesh and season the fish with salt and pepper on both sides. In a large nonstick skillet, heat the olive oil over medium heat and add the fish skin side down. Depending on the thickness of the fish, it might curve on the skillet; if so, use a flat metal spatula to press the skin down. Cook until the fish is cooked through, with the flesh opaque white, 3 to 4 minutes on each side.

Reheat the sauce gently over low heat, stirring vigorously. Add the cilantro.

To serve, arrange the bananas on each plate, place the fish on top, and spoon the sauce around. Garnish with microgreens if you like.

RESTAURANT: Olympe
R. Custódio Serrão, 62 – Lagoa
claudetroisgros.com.br

Frango com Catupiry
CHICKEN WITH CATUPIRY CHEESE SAUCE

Opened in 1934, Bar Lagoa is lit by old-style chandeliers and has dusty floors, wooden tables, and white-haired waiters. Talk about old world. But none of our modern amenities matter when I take in the view, admiring the heart-shaped lake in Rio's Zona Sul, eating this dish, and remembering the days when I used to ride the swan paddle across from the bar.

Brazilians love catupiry cheese. It tastes like butter mixed with fresh cream cheese and a dash of vanilla. While I usually prefer chicken thighs and legs, here catupiry cheese gives chicken breasts glorious tenderness. Serve this with white rice.

SERVES 2–4

1½ pounds boneless, skinless chicken breast halves

Kosher salt and freshly ground black pepper

3 tablespoons extra virgin olive oil

½ small onion, finely chopped

3 scallions chopped, white and green parts

2 garlic cloves, finely minced

2 plum tomatoes, peeled, seeded, and chopped

¼ cup white wine

1 cup chicken stock

1¼ cups catupiry cheese

Preheat the oven to 350°F. Lightly grease a 1-quart baking dish with cooking spray.

Season the chicken with salt and pepper. Heat 2 tablespoons of the olive oil in a large sauté pan over medium heat. Add the chicken, in batches if necessary, and cook, stirring occasionally, until lightly browned, about 4 minutes per side. Transfer the chicken to a plate and cover with foil to keep moist.

Add the remaining 1 tablespoon olive oil to the pan and add the onion and scallions; cook, stirring often, until softened, about 5 minutes. Add the garlic and cook for another minute. Add the tomatoes and cook until the vegetables are softened, about 5 minutes.

Increase the heat to high, add the wine, and bring to a boil, scraping the browned bits from the bottom of the pan.

Add the chicken stock and cook until the sauce has thickened a little, about 3 minutes. Add the cheese and stir to dissolve it in the sauce. Season with salt and pepper.

Cut the chicken crosswise into ½-inch slices and arrange them on the bottom of the prepared baking dish. Pour in any accumulated chicken juices from the plate. Pour the sauce on top of the chicken and bake until hot and bubbling, about 15 minutes. Remove from the oven and cool for 5 minutes before serving.

RESTAURANT: Bar Lagoa,
Av. Epitácio Pessoa, 1674 – Lagoa,
barlagoa.com.br

Sorbet de Cajú
CASHEW FRUIT ICE CREAM

In Rio I've spent many summer nights savoring the bonanza of fruit ice creams at Mil Frutas, a store specializing in exotic fruits from Brazil. This sorbet features a flavor dear to my childhood: cashew fruit. A beautiful mixture of red and orange, cashew fruit's delicious taste is quite different from other fruits, displaying a tannin trait, an astringent woody and pucker feel common in black teas, red wines and other unripe fruits. Because of this quality, the fruit is rarely consumed in its raw state. It is mostly sold in pulps, and featured in juices, ice creams, jellies, drinks, and candies. And then there is the *castanha de cajú*—the cashew nut, of which Brazil is a huge exporter.

MAKES 1 QUART

¼ teaspoon gelatin powder

1 tablespoon plus 1 cup water

1¼ cups sugar

2 tablespoons light corn syrup

2 cups cashew fruit pulp

Few drops of fresh lime or lemon juice

In a small bowl mix the gelatin with 1 tablespoon of water and soak for 3 to 5 minutes.

Meanwhile, place the remaining 1 cup of water, sugar, and corn syrup in a medium saucepan and bring to boil. Cook until the sugar is completely dissolved, 3 to 5 minutes. Remove from the heat and whisk in the gelatin. Allow the syrup to cool at room temperature.

Whisk in the cashew fruit. Taste and adjust the seasoning with a few drops of lime or lemon juice. Chill overnight.

Run the mixture through an ice cream machine according to the manufacturer's instructions until it becomes creamy. Use a rubber spatula to scrape the ice cream into a plastic container (take the time to enjoy some now—freshly out of the machine is my favorite time to eat ice cream). Cover with a tight lid and keep in the freezer for up to 1 month.

RESTAURANT: Mil Frutas, R. Jardim Botânico, 585 – Jardim Botânico, milfrutas.com.br

FLAMENGO
& BOTAFOGO

MODERN CUISINE

This chapter takes us to another lovely neighborhood of Rio: Flamengo and Botafogo (which also happen to be names of soccer teams), where restaurants like Nomangue and Irajá are serving up modern cuisine near the Pão de Açúcar, another landmark situated at nearby Urca.

Brazil is changing, and Rio is changing with it, undergoing a revival and reasserting itself. Since I left Rio in 1997, dining in the city has been getting better all the time, with contemporary trends mixing with Brazilian ingredients. Rio is proof that economic growth and prosperity are precursors to a flourishing cuisine, and the current wave of restaurants in this corner of Rio is a perfect example of this progress. Visit Nomangue and you'll taste another twist on feijoada. The classic black bean stew is a dish you can find all over Rio; shellfish feijoada (page 89), on the other hand, is a unique variation and among Nomangue's

bestselling menu items. At Belmonte, a botequim rooted in this area, hearts of palm soup (page 86) is offered in small bowls before enjoying *petiscos* (finger food). At Irajá the inspiration for cooking molten brigadeiro cake (page 90) is basically the same as making brigadeiro itself: it starts with a mixture of sweetened condensed milk and chocolate, then butter, eggs, and flour are mixed in. I like to serve it with homemade ginger ice cream, but store-bought ice cream is also fine. The result is phenomenal and a taste of Rio itself—always hot, very sexy, and with a spice for life.

SUGAR LOAF

To have a panoramic view of the city, be sure to visit Pão de Açúcar, another breathtaking landmark of Rio. It is connected with a second mountain, Morro da Urca, by cable cars transporting passengers stunned by Rio's beauty. The monument went up in 1912 and today is visited by over a million people per year. Don't forget your camera!

Crème de Palmito
HEARTS OF PALM SOUP

RESTAURANT: Boteco Belmonte
Praia do Flamengo, 300, Flamengo
botecobelmonte.com.br

This is classic botequim food; you will see it all over the menus in Rio. I particularly enjoy the version served at Boteco Belmonte. You can prepare this recipe using canned or jarred hearts of palm, but if you can find fresh hearts of palm (I get them at sos-chefs.com), it's even better. I love this soup because it's healthy, earthy, creamy (without a lot of actual cream), easy to prepare, and simply different. After making it once, I'm sure you'll want to make it often, especially if you have a spare can of hearts of palm in your pantry.

SERVES 4

Seven 4-inch hearts of palm, or one 15-ounce can hearts of palm, drained

2 tablespoons unsalted butter

1 medium onion, roughly chopped

Kosher salt and freshly ground black pepper

2 tablespoons all-purpose flour

2½ cups chicken stock

½ cup heavy cream

1 tablespoon chopped fresh chives

Roughly chop 6 of the hearts of palm; slice the remaining heart of palm and reserve it for garnish.

In a medium saucepan, melt the butter over medium heat and add the onion. Season very lightly with salt and pepper and cook, stirring occasionally with a wooden spoon, until the onion starts to soften, about 3 minutes. Add the hearts of palm and cook for another 2 minutes. Add the flour and cook, stirring constantly, until the flour just starts to lose its flavor, about 2 minutes. Add the chicken stock and bring to a boil. Season lightly with salt and pepper and reduce the heat. Cover and gently simmer until the hearts of palm are softened, about 10 minutes.

Remove the pan from the heat. Working in batches, puree the soup in a blender and return the soup the pan. Add the heavy cream, whisk well, and return to low heat. Bring to a simmer for another 5 minutes (do not let it boil). Adjust the seasonings and divide the soup among bowls; garnish with the sliced heart of palm and the chives.

Rolinho de Rosbife com Rucula, Parmesao e Azeite de Ervas
ROAST BEEF, ARUGULA, AND PARMESAN ROLLS WITH HERBED OLIVE OIL

RESTAURANT: Miam Miam
R. Gen. Góes Monteiro, 34 –
Botafogo, miammiam.com.br

This very simple recipe relies on the quality and freshness of its ingredients. It comes from Roberta Ciasca, chef and owner of Miam Miam, a delightful restaurant that serves comfort Brazilian food with a touch of luxe.

SERVES 4

HERBED OLIVE OIL

1 teaspoon minced shallots

½ teaspoon Dijon mustard

Zest of one lime (or lemon)

1 tablespoon lime juice (from the same lime)

Kosher salt and freshly ground black pepper

4 tablespoons extra virgin olive oil, plus more for drizzling

8 sprigs of thyme, leaves picked and chopped

2 tablespoons chopped fresh parsley

2 tablespoons chopped fresh chives

8 thin slices of roast beef

Kosher salt and freshly ground black pepper

3 ounces baby arugula

One 4-ounce chunk Parmesan cheese

To make the herbed olive oil, combine the shallots, mustard, lime zest and juice, in a bowl. Season with salt and pepper and stir. Slowly add the olive oil, whisking constantly, to emulsify. Add the herbs and mix well.

Working on a clean cutting board, open the roast beef slices and season lightly with salt and pepper. Arrange a few arugula leaves inside each slice, drizzle with some olive oil and season again very lightly with salt and pepper.

Shave the parmesan cheese with a vegetable peeler on top, and roll each slice tight.

Arrange the slices on a platter, drizzle the herbed olive oil on top, and serve.

Feijoada de Frutos de Mar
SHELLFISH FEIJOADA

RESTAURANT: Nomangue,
Estrada Coronel Pedro Correia,
122 lj A, nomangue.com.br

This recipe is inspired by a dish I ate at Nomangue, a restaurant located in Botafogo, a neighborhood in Rio that is now crowded with cool chefs and trendy bistros. The original recipe includes *carne seca* (dried meat), which you braise and then pull apart. I simplified things a bit by leaving it out, as the recipe already calls for an extensive list of proteins. I like to cut the pork into small cubes so it comes out tender but without completely falling apart. Like every good feijoada, Nomangue serves it with a side of white rice and *farofa* (toasted tapioca starch), but to be perfectly honest, I don't feel the need for the side dishes with this version.

SERVES 6-8

1 pound great Northern beans (preferably Goya)

8 ounces pork shoulder, cut into ½-inch cubes

Kosher salt and freshly ground black pepper

5 tablespoons extra virgin olive oil

2 strips of bacon, chopped

1 large linguiça or chorizo (about 7 inches long), sliced

3 garlic cloves, minced

1 onion, finely chopped

4 plum tomatoes, peeled, seeded, and diced

½ teaspoon paprika

Freshly grated nutmeg

8 ounces medium shrimp, peeled and deveined

3 pieces squid, sliced into ¼-inch rings

16 clams, rinsed and scrubbed

12 mussels, rinsed and scrubbed

1 cup dry white wine

¼ cup chopped fresh parsley

Pick any dirt or stones from the beans and quickly rinse them in cold water. Place the beans in a very large pot and cover with cold water (about 10 cups, or at least 2 inches above the beans). Bring to a boil, then reduce the heat to low and cook, covered, until the beans are tender but not mushy, about 40 minutes. Set aside.

Meanwhile, start preparing the meats and vegetables. Season the pork shoulder with salt and pepper. In a large Dutch oven, heat 3 tablespoons of the olive oil over medium heat, add the pork, bacon, and linguiça, and cook, stirring occasionally, until browned, about 5 minutes. Transfer to a bowl and cover tightly with foil. If there is too much fat rendered from the meats, pour some out.

Reduce the heat to low and cook the garlic in the same pan until lightly browned, scraping any browned bits up from the pan. Add the onion and cook, stirring frequently with a wooden spoon, for about 3 minutes. Add the tomatoes, season lightly with salt, pepper, paprika, and nutmeg and cook until well blended, about 2 minutes.

Add the beans and all of their liquid and the meats and simmer over low heat until tender, about 40 minutes.

Meanwhile, season the shrimp and squid with salt and pepper. In a large skillet over medium heat, add the remaining 2 tablespoons olive oil, add the shrimp and squid, and cook until the shrimp just turns orange and the squid turns opaque, 1 to 2 minutes.

In another pan large enough to hold all the shellfish, combine the clams and mussels, pour in the wine, cover the pan, and cook over medium heat until the shells open, shaking the pan occasionally, 5 to 8 minutes. Using a slotted spoon, remove the shellfish and transfer them to the beans, along with the shrimp and squid. Cover and cook, simmering gently for the shellfish to braise with the stew, about 5 minutes. Add more liquid if necessary (water or wine from the shellfish). Adjust the seasonings and serve garnished with the parsley.

Bolinho Quente de Brigadeiro
MOLTEN BRIGADEIRO CAKE

RESTAURANT: Irajá Gastri
Rua Conde de Irajá, 109 –
Botafogo, irajagastro.com.br

Irajá is one of the most exciting restaurants in Rio to open in recent years. Not all of its Brazilian food is traditional, yet none of it feels inauthentic either. There is a serious commitment to Brazilian flavors wedded to international classics and a determination to make ingredients shine. It's as if the chef, Pedro Aragão, has discovered a cuisine all of his own, in which, for example, the most traditional Brazilian sweet, brigadeiro, turns into a hot chocolate cake. I decided to take the idea a little further and came up with a molten brigadeiro cake with an irresistible flow of melted fudge, perfect for Brazilians (especially me) who can't wait until their brigadeiro has cooled before indulging!

SERVES 6

½ cup (1 stick) unsalted butter, plus more for the molds

¼ cup all-purpose flour, sifted, plus more for the molds

One 14-ounce can sweetened condensed milk

1 teaspoon unsweetened cocoa powder

2 ounces 70% dark chocolate, chopped

2 large eggs

2 large egg yolks

⅛ teaspoon salt

1 tablespoon sugar

1 teaspoon vanilla extract

SPECIAL EQUIPMENT:
6 individual foil cups

COOKING TIP: It's frustrating when a cake doesn't come out of the pan properly, with part of it still clinging, so a word of advice: butter and flour the pan very well. Use softened butter—not melted—and shake off the excess flour.

Preheat the oven to 350°F. Butter and flour the foil cups (see Tip).

In a medium heavy saucepan, combine the condensed milk, cocoa powder, and chocolate and bring to a boil over medium heat, whisking constantly. When the mixture begins to bubble and the chocolate melts, reduce the heat to low and continue whisking for another 3 to 5 minutes, until the mixture has thickened like fudge. You should be able to tilt the pan and the whole batter will slide, leaving the sticky fudge on the bottom of the pan. Slide the batter into a large bowl without scraping it, as you don't want to incorporate any of the thick residue left on the bottom of the pan.

In a separate medium saucepan, melt the butter over low heat. Pour the butter into the chocolate mixture and whisk vigorously until smooth. At first it will curdle and break, and you will think this recipe cannot possibly work; don't despair, and keep whisking constantly until the mixture comes together again.

In a separate bowl, beat together the eggs, yolks, salt, sugar, and vanilla and add it to the chocolate mixture, whisking until incorporated.

Add the flour and mix it in with a rubber spatula until just blended.

Pour the batter into the prepared foil cups, filling them to about ¼ inch from the top. You can prepare the recipe up to this point, cover, and refrigerate for up to 5 days; bring to room temperature before baking.

Bake for 7 to 9 minutes, until the edges are firm but the center is still soft. Invert onto a dessert plate. Serve with ice cream (pistachio, ginger, coconut, and vanilla all work well with this dessert).

SANTA TEREZA,
GLÓRIA, LARANJEIRAS
& CÓSME VELHO

SANTA TERESA, GLÓRIA, LARANJEIRAS & COSME VELHO: DINING WITH A VIEW

Rio offers so many gorgeous landmarks. The city is built between the ocean and mountains and the result is urban beauty so intense, so electrifying, that we cariocas applaud it any chance we get. Visit Christ the Redeemer and you feel like you're on the top of the world. And the question I usually ask myself when I am up there and the sun is burning upon the blue skies is: Where should I dine when the night descends?

If this question is on your mind too, and if you like to dine with a view, may I suggest Aprazível, located in Santa Teresa, not too far from the Christ in Cosme Velho. It inspired me to prepare a similar version of *galinhada* (a chicken rice dish; page 102) that is simple and beautiful, just like the restaurant. Or perhaps you can try Bar do Mineiro, where the food and the mood represent Rio in each bite, inspiring the recipe for *sopa de feijão* (page 96).

Once in Santa Teresa, be sure to visit Alda Maria Doces Portugueses, a Portuguese pastry shop, and you'll go back in time. The furniture and china are all from Portugal and so are the sweets. Alda shared her recipe for *ovos moles* (page 106), a treat that has been enjoyed for more than two hundred years. Oh, those Portuguese sweets! Growing up in Rio,

I was destined to love them. Ever since I can remember, I have been hooked on the blissfully rich taste of the eggy pastries of Portuguese cuisine.

One of the greatest pleasures of writing this book was discovering a whole range of talented cooks who don't have restaurants. Among them, I found Manuela Arraes and her partner, Monica Verdial (also see Elvira Bona, page 61), who, like many other talented women, feed an industry that moves millions of Reais (that's our Brazilian currency) every year as part of the "informal economy," working as caterers for parties and events, producing thousands of delicacies from incredibly simple stoves. The flavors coming out of their kitchens inspired some of the recipes in this chapter. Try a baked salt cod casserole (page 102), followed by an orange roulade (page 108), and you'll have a Portuguese feast at home.

On Saturdays you can visit the farmers' market Feira da Glória and shop like a carioca. Talk to the vendors and ask them how they prepare their food at home. I took cues from lots of street vendors to write this book. They inspired some recipes, like *tomatada* (page 98), and some are entirely my own creation, like the green bean salad (page 101), which highlights the sweetness of green beans in an elegant presentation. Whether you choose to use these recipes as everyday meals or for a special occasion, they are a fun way to bring Rio's flavors to your table.

CHRIST THE REDEEMER

This famous statue of Rio was the brainchild of a carioca engineer, Heitor da Silva Costa (1823–1947), who proposed it in 1921 and received help with its construction from French-Polish sculptor Paul Landowski (1875–1961). The 130-foot-high monument stands on top of Corcovado Mountain and depicts Jesus Christ with open arms. It was unveiled in October 1931, and at the time, the project caused quite a dispute over the religious image of Christ. But today Christ the Redeemer transcends any religious representation—it is viewed as a work of art, as an engineering victory, and a tourist landmark. More than a symbol of faith, Christ the Redeemer is a symbol of Rio and of Brazil, and he can be seen hugging and blessing the city from almost any corner of Rio. It is a geographic point of reference, but to me just as important, when I look up at him I always think he is casting a mysterious spell over me composed of equal parts adrenaline and peace, making me feel very lucky to be a carioca.

Sopa de Feijão com Salsicha
BLACK BEAN AND SAUSAGE SOUP

RESTAURANT: Bar Mineiro
R. Paschoal Carlos Magno, 99 –
Santa Teresa, bardomineiro.net

Let me make a confession to you: while I was born and raised in Rio, I now live in the suburbs of Connecticut. Many times when I look outside the window, all I see is a squirrel munching on an acorn, surrounded by naked trees under a bucolic scenery of gray lights and cloudy skies. Even though New York City is right in my backyard (just an hour from home), assimilating with the local American culture can be difficult at times. I often long for the warm sunny days of my hometown, people crowding the streets, doormen who stop cleaning the boardwalk to admire the beautiful women passing by. But even more than that, I miss the spirit of Rio, which I remember clearly at Bar Mineiro, eating feijoada, a large, boisterous meal on the plate.

Out of spiritual necessity, I've had to find a way to come up with a feijoada-inspired dish without all the planning ahead. My attachment to black beans means that they are a staple in my pantry. As a good carioca, this comes with another attachment, to a pressure cooker, and that's how I always cook my beans (but you can use canned beans as well). I usually use the first sausage I can grab (linguiça is my favorite, chorizo comes second, fresh sausage comes third) to make this carioca soup in a jiff.

SERVES 4

2 tablespoons extra virgin olive oil, plus more if needed

8 ounces linguiça sausage or chorizo

3 garlic cloves, finely minced

½ onion, finely chopped

2 scallions, white and green parts, chopped

2 plum tomatoes, peeled, seeded, and chopped

1 teaspoon dried oregano

Kosher salt and freshly ground black pepper

1½ cups chicken stock

1½ cups cooked black beans or one 15-ounce can black beans

2 tablespoons chopped fresh parsley

Heat the olive oil in a large skillet over medium-low heat. Remove the linguiça from the cases and add it in chunks to the pan, breaking it up with a wooden spoon. Cook the linguiça until just starting to brown, about 3 minutes. Using a slotted spoon, transfer the linguiça to a bowl and cover to keep moist.

Using the same pan and adding a little more oil if necessary, add the garlic and cook until lightly browned, then add the onion and scallions and cook until softened, about 5 minutes.

Add the tomatoes and oregano, reduce the heat to low, and continue cooking until all the ingredients are softened, about 2 minutes. Season lightly with salt and pepper. Add the stock, increase the heat, and bring to a boil. Add the beans, linguiça, and any juices that have accumulated in the bowl and bring to a boil again; immediately reduce the heat to a simmer, taste, and adjust the seasoning. Partially cover and cook for 10 to 15 minutes to meld the flavors. Sprinkle with the parsley and serve immediately.

Tomatada
PLUM TOMATO AND BREAD SOUP

I love the name of this soup: *tomatada*. Even though it might sound like a late-night fight, tomatada is nothing more salacious than tomato and bread soup, prepared in the Portuguese style. By that I mean *acordas*—bread added to soups and stews (see Acorda Alantejana on page 54). This recipe comes from a Portuguese vendor at the farmers' market Feira da Glória, who told me how his wife makes *tomatada* at home for their family, and it's one I like to make in summer when I have tons of tomatoes at hand.

SERVES 4

2 cups bread, cut into ½-inch cubes

4 tablespoons extra virgin olive oil

Kosher salt and freshly ground black pepper

1 teaspoon white wine vinegar

4 large eggs

½ red onion, finely chopped

1 garlic clove, smashed and finely minced

4 plum tomatoes, peeled, seeded, and roughly chopped

4 cups chicken stock

3 cups packed fresh cilantro leaves

Preheat the oven to 350°F. Place the bread cubes in a bowl and drizzle 1 tablespoon of the olive oil on top. Season with salt and pepper and toss. Spread on a baking sheet and toast in the oven until just beginning to get crisp, 5 to 10 minutes, mixing once halfway through. Remove from the oven and set aside.

Bring a pot of water to a simmer and have a bowl of iced water nearby. Add the vinegar to the simmering water and mix well. Break each egg into a cup or ramekin and gently lower the eggs into the simmering water, coming as close as you can to the water. Poach the eggs until the whites are set but the yolks remain runny, 3 to 4 minutes. Using a slotted spoon, transfer the eggs one at a time to a plate. Cover loosely with foil or a lid.

In a large saucepan, heat the remaining 3 tablespoons olive oil over low heat and add the onion; cook until softened, about 3 minutes. Add the garlic, stir, and cook for 1 minute. Add the tomatoes and cook, stirring occasionally, until they start to soften, about 2 minutes. Add the chicken stock, stirring with a wooden spoon, and bring to a simmer. Season with salt and pepper. Add the cilantro leaves just before serving.

Distribute the cubed bread and eggs among 4 soup bowls, ladle the soup on top, and serve.

Abobrinha Frita da Rita

RITA'S FRIED ZUCCHINI

Rita de Cassia Pereira da Silva is a carioca home cook with several signature recipes in her repertoire. This fried zucchini dish is one of them (*carne moída*, page 188, is another). She serves it as a side dish, but I find it to be so irresistibly crunchy and salty that I often eat the whole thing and call it a meal.

SERVES 4

1½ pounds zucchini (about 4 medium)

Kosher salt and freshly ground black pepper

2 cups vegetable oil for frying

1 cup all-purpose flour

Trim the top and bottom of the zucchini. Cut them in half, then cut into sticks about ¼ inch thick and 3 to 4 inches long. Place the zucchini sticks in a colander set inside a bowl. Sprinkle with salt and set aside for at least 20 minutes and preferably 1 hour for the zucchini to release its water. Transfer to a plate lined with a double thickness of paper towels and pat dry to remove any remaining moisture.

Meanwhile, pour the oil into a large skillet and heat over medium-high heat to 350°F as measured on a deep-fry thermometer.

While the oil is heating, pour the flour into a bowl and season with salt and pepper. Toss the zucchini sticks in the flour until they are completely covered in flour. Using your hands, shake the zucchini ever so lightly to remove some of the excess flour. If you shake in a strainer or colander, too much flour will fall off the zucchini—you don't want that. If some of the zucchini starts to absorb the flour while you're frying, toss the remaining zucchini generously in flour again just before frying.

When the oil is ready, slip half of the zucchini sticks into the oil, being careful not to crowd the pan. Fry until golden brown and crisp, about 4 minutes, moving the sticks around occasionally with a slotted spoon. Transfer to a plate covered with paper towels. Repeat with the remaining zucchini. Sprinkle with salt and serve immediately.

Vagem com Minas e Castanha do Pará

GREEN BEANS WITH MINAS CHEESE AND BRAZIL NUTS

Summer in Rio is no joke, with temperatures normally in the nineties and sometimes getting up to above one hundred. People are exercising at the beach, the scent of coconut water covers the boardwalk, soccer is at the Estádio do Maracanã, and then more soccer on television. People are packing their *cangas* (a cloth that serves as a beach towel), their sunglasses, and *sandalias havaianas* (our version of flip-flops) and heading straight to the beach. This is my Rio, the perfect time to eat vegetable salads and fresh cheeses with refreshing flavors. I prepared this recipe using green beans I bought at the farmers' market Feira da Glória after a morning at the beach and a juice at a juice bar.

SERVES 4

1½ pounds string beans, ends trimmed

Kosher salt and freshly ground black pepper

2 tablespoons fresh lime juice

1 teaspoon soy sauce

1 garlic clove, minced

½ cup extra virgin olive oil

½ cup crumbled Minas cheese

¼ cup thinly sliced red onion

⅓ cup Brazil nuts

Fill a large bowl with ice and water. Place the green beans in a steamer or a pot fitted with a steaming basket over boiling water. Season with salt, cover the steamer, and steam until just tender, about 5 minutes. Transfer the beans to the ice water bath for 5 minutes to cool. Remove the green beans from the water using a slotted spoon and spread them on a plate covered with paper towels to absorb any extra water. Let air dry for 5 minutes, then place them in a serving bowl.

In a medium bowl, whisk together the lime juice, soy sauce, garlic, and salt and pepper to taste. While whisking, slowly add the olive oil until well blended.

Pour enough dressing over to coat lightly (reserve the rest for another use). Add the cheese and red onion and grate the Brazil nuts over the green beans with a Microplane. Taste, adjust the seasonings, and serve.

Galinhada
CHICKEN AND CHORIZO OVER JASMINE RICE

RESTAURANT: R. Aprazível, 62 – Santa Teresa, aprazivel.com.br

If you like to see things from up high, you must visit Santa Teresa, a bohemian neighborhood bordering Cosme Velho, where the divine Cristo is located. The arrival in Santa Teresa is gorgeous, especially if you come through the Arcos da Lapa. The *bondinho* (trolley) is the symbol of the place, and in the center of Santa Teresa is Largo do Guimarães, where everything happens, where you'll find trendy boutiques, bars, and restaurants. From the rustic chic tables of the stylish restaurant Aprazível, your view of Ponte Rio Niterói stretches before your eyes while you enjoy a delicious *galinhada*. There it is served with many side dishes, including beans, plantains, and collard greens, but I decided to focus on the *galinhada* alone—in essence chicken and rice cooked together—for a dish that is easy to prepare at home.

SERVES 6–8

3 whole garlic cloves

2 teaspoons kosher salt

2 tablespoons fresh lime juice

2 teaspoons dried oregano

1 whole chicken, skin on (3 to 4 pounds), cut into 8 pieces

Freshly ground black pepper

3 tablespoons olive oil

3 ounces Spanish chorizo, cut into ¼-inch-thick slices

2 medium onions, diced

3 scallions, green and white parts, chopped

3 large garlic cloves, minced

2 teaspoons chopped fresh thyme

1 teaspoon paprika

2 fresh bay leaves

1 pound plum tomatoes, peeled, seeded, and diced

2 cups long-grain white rice, preferably Jasmine

2½ cups chicken stock

2 tablespoons unsalted butter

¼ cup chopped fresh parsley

Mince and mash the whole garlic cloves to a paste with the salt, then transfer to a large bowl. Stir in the lime juice and oregano. Add the chicken pieces and rub all over with the marinade until well coated. Cover with plastic wrap and leave at room temperature for 1 hour.

Spread the chicken over a baking sheet covered with paper towels and pat dry. Season with pepper on all sides.

In a large heavy sauté pan, heat 2 tablespoons of the olive oil over medium heat. Add the chicken skin side down and cook until lightly browned all over, about 3 minutes per side. Using a slotted spoon, transfer the chicken to a bowl and cover with foil to keep it moist.

If there is too much fat in the pan, drain a little. If there is a lot of garlic stuck to the pan, deglaze with about ½ cup water, scraping the bottom of the pan, and bring to a boil. Strain into a bowl and set aside.

Heat the remaining 1 tablespoon olive oil in the same pan over medium heat, add the chorizo, and cook until lightly browned on both sides, about 2 minutes per side. Using a slotted spoon, transfer the chorizo to the bowl with the chicken. Cover again.

Keeping the fat that's left in the pan, reduce the heat to low, add the onions and scallions, and cook until softened, stirring occasionally with a wooden spoon and scraping the bottom of the pan, about 2 minutes. Add the minced garlic and cook for another minute. Add the thyme, paprika, bay leaves, and tomatoes and cook until the tomatoes are softened, 4 to 5 minutes. Add the rice and stir well, making sure every grain is shiny and well mixed into the vegetable mixture. (If you would like to add the deglazing juices from the chicken, now is the time.) Then add the stock and bring to a boil. Reduce the heat to low and add the chicken, sausage, and any juice that accumulated in the bowl, arranging it all evenly over the rice. Season with salt and pepper, cover, and cook gently until the rice has absorbed all the liquid, 20 to 30 minutes.

Stir in the butter gently and serve, garnished with the parsley.

Bacalhau de Natas

SALT COD, YOUNG POTATOES, AND BELL PEPPERS WITH BÉCHAMEL SAUCE

This recipe comes from Manuela Arraes (you can read more about her on page 108). The word *nata* in Portuguese refers to cream of milk, or heavy cream. In this dish, however, it refers to the creamy béchamel sauce that goes on top of the salt cod. If you would like to keep this dish on the lighter side, skip the béchamel sauce completely, but because the sauce does not really penetrate the fish and vegetable layer; even if you keep the béchamel, the outcome will still be on the light side. A glass of white wine is the perfect drink companion.

SERVES 8

1¾ pounds dried salt cod

2½ cups cold milk

2 pounds small new potatoes

Kosher salt

½ cup plus 3 tablespoons extra virgin olive oil

2 medium onions, thinly sliced

1 red bell pepper, cored, seeded, and thinly sliced

1 yellow bell pepper, cored, seeded, and thinly sliced

1 green bell pepper, cored, seeded, and thinly sliced

4 garlic cloves, finely minced

¼ cup chopped fresh parsley

½ cup freshly grated Parmesan cheese

BÉCHAMEL SAUCE

1 cup milk, plus 2 cups of the poaching milk from the cod

5 tablespoons unsalted butter

5 tablespoons all-purpose flour

Kosher salt and freshly ground black pepper

Freshly grated nutmeg

Pinch of cayenne pepper

Rinse the salt cod in cold water and place inside a large container. Fill with about 2½ gallons water (the volume of water should be 10 to 15 times the size of the cod). Store in the refrigerator to soak overnight, changing the water at least 3 times a day.

Transfer the fish to a medium saucepan (cut the fish if necessary). Cover the fish with the cold milk. Bring to a boil, then reduce the heat to low and cook, covered, until opaque, 15 to 20 minutes. Turn the heat off and let the cod rest in the milk, covered, for at least 20 minutes. Using a slotted spoon, remove the cod, strain the milk and set aside. Flake the fish with your hands into small chunks, or pulse in a food processor for just a few seconds, being careful not to shred it too much (you can keep the shredded cod for up to 12 hours in the refrigerator before using).

Place the potatoes in a large heavy saucepan and cover with cold water by at least 1 inch. Add a large pinch of salt and bring to a boil. Reduce the heat to medium and simmer until fork-tender, 12 to 15 minutes. Drain the potatoes and spread them on a plate. When cool enough to handle, peel and slice the potatoes ¼ inch thick. Set aside.

Heat 3 tablespoons of the olive oil in a large skillet over low heat. Add the onions and peppers and cook, stirring occasionally, until softened, 10 to 15 minutes. Add the garlic and cook for 1 minute. Mix in the shredded cod and parsley, cover, and set aside.

Preheat the oven to 350°F and lightly grease a 9 x 13-inch baking dish with cooking spray.

To make the béchamel sauce, heat the fresh and reserved milk in a medium saucepan over low heat. In another medium saucepan, melt the butter over low heat. Add the flour, and cook, stirring constantly with a wooden spoon, until it foams. Pour in the milk and cook, whisking constantly, until the sauce thickens. Taste, as the milk will be salty from the cod, then season with salt, pepper, nutmeg, and cayenne.

Lay half of the potatoes across the prepared baking dish in a single layer. Spread half of the cod mixture on top evenly. Repeat with another layer of potatoes and cod. Drizzle the remaining ½ cup olive oil all over and ladle the béchamel sauce on top (the sauce will not penetrate the dish). Sprinkle with the cheese and bake until bubbly and golden brown, about 25 minutes. Serve hot.

Mousse de Maracujá
PASSION FRUIT MOUSSE

It's still dusk in Rio when the men arranging the stands at the farmers' market Feira da Glória arrive with their trucks loaded with fruit. As you enter the neighborhood you can feel the bright yellow gold light that slants onto each stand, and the passion fruit mirrors that same yellow light for a moment of magic. At Feira da Glória, the passion fruit is loaded with pulp, crowded with black seeds, and bursting with wet juices. When I am back home in Rio, I find myself using passion fruit in sauces, salads, and ice cream and generally making it part of my weekly cooking routine. Passion fruit mousse, creamy and tart, fluffy and silky, never leaves my Rio cooking routine, even as other recipes may come and go. When I am not in Rio, I use frozen pulp, which you can find in most supermarket frozen food aisles, and I am plenty satisfied with the results.

SERVES 8–10

2½ teaspoons (1 envelope) powdered gelatin

¼ cup water

One 14-ounce sweetened condensed milk

1⅓ cups plus 3 tablespoons passion-fruit puree, thawed

¾ cup heavy cream

3 large egg whites

Pinch of salt

1 to 2 tablespoons sugar

In a small saucepan, stir the gelatin into the water and set aside for 3 to 5 minutes.

Meanwhile, combine the sweetened condensed milk and passion fruit puree in a blender and blend until homogenous.

Warm the gelatin over low heat (don't boil), pour into the blender with the passion fruit, and blend for 1 minute. Transfer to a bowl.

In the bowl of a mixer fitted with the whisk attachment, whip the heavy cream to medium peaks. Set aside.

In another mixer bowl fitted with a clean whisk attachment, start beating the egg whites with the salt at medium speed. As they start to foam, gradually add the sugar, increasing the speed, until soft peaks form.

Using a spatula, carefully fold the whipped cream into the passion fruit mousse, then fold in the egg whites.

Using a ladle or a measuring spoon with a spout, pour the mixture into wine glasses, cover with plastic, and refrigerate for at least 6 hours before serving.

ALDA MARIA TALAVERA CAMPOS

Alda Maria Talavera Campos is an eighth-generation Portuguese sweet maker, or *doceira,* as we say in Portuguese. She was born in Pelotas, a city in the state of Rio Grande do Sul with a reputation built upon Portuguese sweets. From the time she was a toddler, she remembers nothing but baking and watching her mother and grandmother produce sweets such as compotes, preserved fruit, and all kinds of egg yolk-based custards.

Alda got married at a very young age and had three kids, but soon found herself divorced with a family to support all by herself. "I raised my kids making sweets," Alda told me. She moved to Porto Alegre (the capital of that state) and had no trouble finding a job as a *doceira*. Years later, Alda met and fell in love with a young carioca musician, who showed her Rio and its major Portuguese influence. She then moved to Rio and opened her store in 2003. Alda's two daughters, Simone and Liliana—the ninth generation—are already in the kitchen helping their mother grow the business. And then there is Laura, Liliana's two-year-old daughter, whose love for baking Portuguese sweets is clearly in her blood.

Ovos Moles de Aveiro
SWEET EGG YOLK CUSTARD

SHOP: Alda Maria Doces Portugueses
R. Alm. Alexandrino, 1116 – Santa
Teresa, aldadoceportugueses.com.br

Alda Maria Doces Portugueses is one of those rare shops that takes you back in time. You feel like you are in a past century with furniture, china, and sweets that lived through more than two hundred years of tradition. The proud owner, Alda (read more about her at left), shared this recipe for *ovos moles de aveiro* with me. As old as the convents of Portugal, *ovos moles de aveiro* is one of the most iconic sweets of Portuguese cuisine and one of the most popular sweets at the store. It can also be used as filling for cakes and cookies, but eaten plain—the way Alda serves it—is Portuguese culinary heaven.

SERVES 6

1½ cups sugar

⅓ cup water

12 large egg yolks

½ tablespoon unsalted butter

SPECIAL EQUIPMENT:
Six to eight 2-ounce ramekins

Place the sugar and water in a medium saucepan and bring to a boil over high heat without stirring. Cook just until the sugar is dissolved, about 3 minutes. Remove from the heat and let sit, without touching or stirring, for 15 minutes.

While whisking, slowly pour the yolks into the sugar syrup, scraping every drop of yolk into the syrup. Add the butter and continue to whisk. Now get ready to babysit this custard: cook it over the lowest heat, stirring constantly with a wooden spoon. In the beginning there will be a light foam, then, as the custard thickens, the foam will disappear. Continue to cook the custard until thickened, about 10 minutes. You are looking for custard that is thicker than vanilla sauce but thinner than vanilla pudding. (As soon as you see the first bubble, it's time to take it out.) Set a fine strainer over a medium bowl. Immediately scrape and push the custard through the strainer. Do not stir the strained custard. Cool it to room temperature without mixing or touching. Don't try to accelerate the chilling process with an ice bath or immediate refrigeration; for a smooth texture, let it cool at room temperature, then chill for at least 6 hours or overnight—still no mixing. (At this point you can keep the custard in a container with a tight-fitting lid for up to 20 days in the refrigerator.)

Remove the bowl from the refrigerator. If there is any crystallization, carefully scrape and discard it. Using a tablespoon, scoop a small mound (about 2 ounces) of custard into each ramekin. Serve slightly chilled or at room temperature.

Rocambole de Laranja
ROULADE WITH ORANGE-CARAMEL SAUCE

Manuela Arraes (or Naná to most cariocas) is a beautiful Portuguese woman who immigrated to Rio de Janeiro when she was sixteen years old. She made a life for herself in the pastry business, and today many Brazilians consider her (and her business partner, Monica Soares Verdial) among the best Portuguese bakers in the country. Recently they invited me for a lunch cooked by Naná, with this delicious roulade as dessert. She prefers to use store-bought fresh orange juice instead of juicing the oranges herself—she says store-bought has a stronger taste—so I followed her directions.

SERVES 8–10

12 large eggs

3 cups sugar, plus more for rolling

2 cups store-bought fresh orange juice

½ cup all-purpose flour

Zest of 3 oranges (preferably navel, save the oranges to section for garnish)

ORANGE-CARAMEL SAUCE

½ cup sugar

2 tablespoons water

1 cup fresh orange juice

Preheat the oven to 350°F. Grease a 12 x 18 x 2-inch baking sheet with butter, line it with parchment paper, and grease the parchment. Have a clean kitchen towel and some sugar handy.

Combine the eggs and sugar in the bowl of an electric mixer. Set the bowl over a pan of simmering water (without touching the water) and heat just until lukewarm to the touch, whisking constantly with a long whisk to prevent curdling. Bring the bowl to the mixer and attach the whisk. Start beating on low speed, gradually increasing to high, and beat until thickened, whitened, and tripled in volume, 10 to 12 minutes.

Meanwhile, in a medium bowl, whisk the orange juice with the flour, making sure there are no lumps. Add the zest and whisk again.

Using a rubber spatula, in 3 small additions, pour the orange juice mixture into the egg mixture, carefully folding from the bottom up and trying not to deflate it too much. Pour into the prepared baking sheet.

Bake for 25 to 30 minutes, rotating once halfway through, until puffed, lightly browned, and the cake is just starting to pull away from the sides. Transfer the pan to a wire rack and let rest for 5 to 10 minutes. (You want to work with the roulade while still warm, or it won't stick.)

Wet a kitchen towel completely, twist, and wring out excess water. Stretch the towel on a clean counter and dust generously with sugar. Invert the roulade onto the towel, remove the pan, and carefully peel off the parchment paper. If the edges are too dark, you might want to trim them slightly, or they will leave a dark trace inside the roulade.

Roll the cake so that the short side is closest to you—be careful as you want to roll tightly without breaking it. Be sure to leave the seam on the bottom. Trim the two outer sides to make a clean cut. Let cool to room temperature, then transfer to a plate using a long spatula.

Meanwhile, make the sauce: In a medium saucepan, combine the sugar and water and cook over high heat until a light brown caramel forms. Carefully add the orange juice; it will splash. Cook, whisking constantly over low heat, until well blended, 3 to 5 minutes. Strain through a fine sieve into a bowl. Serve with the roulade and orange sections on the side.

COOKING TIP: I didn't have to change a thing on the recipe—it adapted perfectly to my American kitchen—but I jazz it up a little by serving it with orange sections and an orange-caramel sauce, whereas Naná serves it plain. You could also serve it with a good orange jam on the side or simply garnished with orange peel.

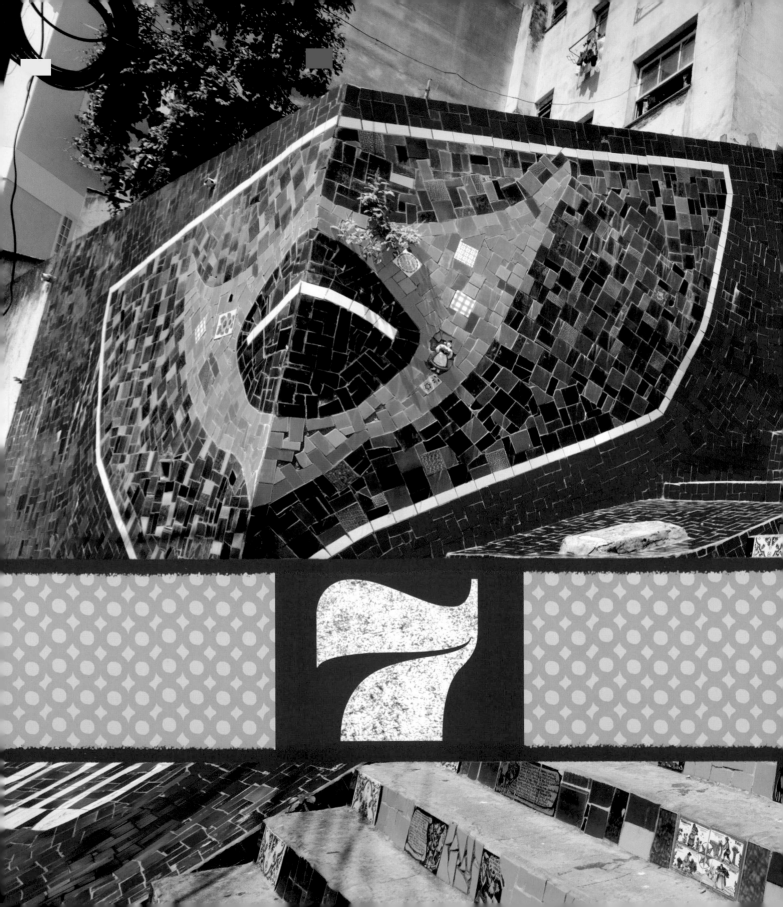

CENTRO, LAPA
& ARREDORES

CENTRO, LAPA & ARREDORES: SAMBA & CULINARY TWISTS

Rio is the city of samba. And in this chapter you will find recipes that will make you samba—I promise! It's here, in downtown Rio, that samba is practiced by sambistas and composers and at samba schools. The whole country stops for Carnival, the biggest party on earth. The parade happens downtown, at Avenida Marquês de Sapucaí. In all of Rio, there is no place with the energy of the Sambodromo (the area of samba) during Carnival, where there is a constellation of beautiful women and an explosion of music and dancing. Taking part in Carnival in Rio is one of the most joyful experiences you can have.

Sometimes, all it takes to feel transported to the city of samba is a recipe. A twist over a classic: that's what Kátia Barbosa did when she created *bolinho de feijoada* (page 114), a dish that took Brazil by storm. (Another one of Kátia's highlights is the pork ribs with guava glaze and polenta turnovers on page 122.)

Downtown has another important identity: it is the business and finance center, where political and economic decisions are made. I remember the days when I worked in finance in downtown Rio, all dressed up and going for lunches with men in suits. But my favorite part of lunch was the food. I would often suggest

restaurant O Navegador just so that I could eat *pudim de claras* (page 126).

Once in a while business lunches would be held at a botequim. The leg of lamb from Nova Capela (page 119) is a recipe that draws people from all over town, as if the restaurant is fated to do little else, even though everything else is great. Other carioca botequims inspired the recipes in this chapter. Try a *bife à milanesa* based on one by botequim Bar Luíz (page 121) or *pudim de tapioca* (page 127) when you want a break from the traditional *pudim de leite*.

CARNIVAL

The word *carnival* comes from the Latin word *carnelevament*, which means "remove the meat." Nobody knows for sure the origin of Carnival. Some say that it started in BC as a way to celebrate good harvest times. Around the seventh century, Carnival was made official in Greece to celebrate the god of wine. It was at that time that Carnival started to be associated with alcohol and eroticism, and its popularity grew so much that the church could not contain it and made it official.

Carnival was brought to Brazil during colonization and was called Entrudo. But only after the Africans introduced their own touch was the Brazilian Carnival born as we know it today. Carnival opened a new industry to music, travel, parties, costumes, and commerce.

Of all the Carnivals around the world, none is as grand and euphoric as the one in Rio de Janeiro. This is a well-organized event, and it lasts for four days, starting on a Sunday and ending on Ash Wednesday, when the final samba winner is announced. The samba schools start rehearsing months before Carnival, each representing a particular theme and regulated by strict rules, all dancing for the winning title.

Bolinho de Feijoada do Aconchego Carioca

FEIJOADA FRITTERS WITH COLLARD GREENS

Kátia Barbosa, the chef at Aconchego Carioca, an exciting botequim located near Praça da Bandeira, is playing with the most traditional dishes of Brazilian cuisine and creating new classics. If you are a tourist, you might never have heard of the neighborhood Praça da Bandeira, but trust me, you want to go there. The food being served at Aconchego Carioca is captivating audiences from all over town and fueling the renaissance of a whole neighborhood.

I heard a lot about Kátia's famous feijoada fritters, so when I first tried them, I was full of expectations. Well, let me tell you that this *bolinho* (fritter) exceeded them: it is a bright twist on our national dish, one that offers a tiny crunchy taste of our traditional black bean and meat stew. Serve with orange sections and a caipirinha.

MAKES ABOUT 40

1 pound dried black beans (about 2¼ cups), picked and rinsed

4 ounces jerk meat (*carne seca*, see Glossary), cut into ½-inch cubes

4 ounces pork shoulder, cut into ½-inch cubes

4 ounces bacon, cut into thin strips

1 linguiça (or chorizo), cut into ½-inch cubes

3 bay leaves

8 cups water

2 tablespoons extra virgin olive oil

5 garlic cloves, finely minced

Kosher salt and freshly ground black pepper

Pinch of cayenne

Pinch of paprika

Freshly grated nutmeg

1 cup manioc flour (*farinha de mandioca fina*)

2 tablespoons sour manioc starch (*povilho azedo*)

4 cups vegetable oil, for frying

Combine the beans, jerk meat, pork, bacon, linguiça, and bay leaves inside a pressure cooker. Pour in the water, cover the pan, lock the lid, and cook until the beans are soft and the meat is tender, about 1 hour (start at high; when you hear the pressure hissing, bring the heat down to low and start timing). Remove the steam/pressure, uncover the pan, and cool for 20 minutes. (If you don't have a pressure cooker, put the ingredients in a Dutch oven pan and cook for 3 hours, until the beans and meat are cooked.)

Transfer everything to a blender and blend until smooth—do this in batches if necessary. At this point the mixture will look like a thick brown paste—not very appealing, but stay with me, it really will taste divine.

In a large skillet, heat the olive oil over medium heat, add the garlic, and cook until just golden, about 2 minutes. Add the bean and meat paste, reduce the heat to low, and cook, stirring with a wooden spoon, until it starts to bubble, 5 to 8 minutes. Taste (it will be quite seasoned from the meats) and adjust the seasoning with salt, pepper, the cayenne, paprika, and nutmeg.

Sprinkle in 1 cup of the manioc flour, stirring with a wooden spoon until the bean puree starts to pull from the pan, leaving a skin on the bottom, about 5 minutes. Transfer to a bowl and let cool slightly.

Sprinkle the sour manioc starch on a cool surface and knead the bean paste with the starch until well combined and smooth. Transfer to a large bowl and cover loosely with plastic wrap to keep it moist.

To make the collard greens, in a separate large skillet, heat the olive oil over medium heat and add the bacon, cooking until just crisp, about 3 minutes. Add the garlic and cook for 1 minute, just until crispy. Add the blanched collard greens and toss, stirring constantly, until tender, about 5 minutes. Transfer to a plate and cool to room temperature.

Scoop about 2 tablespoons of the bean paste and roll it into a ball. Using your thumb, press a cavity into the ball, stuff with a small amount of the collard green mixture, and close the ball, pinching to seal. Lightly press the ball between your hands to form it into a patty shape, making sure the filling is completely enclosed. Repeat with the remaining bean paste and collards. (At this point, the feijoada fritters can be covered and refrigerated for up to 2 hours before cooking, or frozen for up to

RESTAURANT: Aconchego
Carioca, Rua Barao de Iguatemi,
379 Praça da Bandeira,
aconchegocarioca.com.br

COLLARD GREENS

1 tablespoon olive oil

8 ounces bacon, finely diced

2 garlic cloves

1 bunch collard greens, sliced very thin and blanched

INGREDIENT NOTE: Just like feijoada (page 38), you can use different kinds of meat here. Try to include different flavors, like smoked meats, fresh meats, and different sausages.

6 months; freeze in a single layer on a parchment paper–lined baking sheet, then transfer to freezer bags.)

Pour the vegetable oil into a heavy-bottomed pot and heat to 350°F, as measured by a deep-fat thermometer. Fry the fritters in batches, adding as many as will fit without touching, turning them occasionally with a long slotted spoon. They will not take on a lot of color; they will become just a shade darker after frying. Transfer to a plate covered with paper towels. Continue working in batches until all are fried. (The fritters can be kept in an airtight container in the fridge and reheated in a 300°F oven for 5 to 10 minutes.)

Sopa Leão Veloso

SHRIMP, MUSSEL, AND SQUID SOUP WITH SHREDDED WHITE FISH AND FRESH PARSLEY

RESTAURANT: Rio Minho
R. do Ouvidor, 10 – Centro

Minho is the name of a river in Portugal, and *rio* is the word for river; Rio Minho is a fitting name for the oldest restaurant in Rio de Janeiro. Created in 1884 by Portuguese immigrants, one of the specialties is *sopa leão veloso*. This dish was named for a Brazilian minister of international relations, Pedro Leão Veloso Neto (1887–1947), who during his many travels fell in love with bouillabaisse in France. Back in Rio—in those days the capital of Brazil—he handed the recipe to the owners of Rio Minho and asked them to recreate it. But bouillabaisse is a hard word for Brazilians to pronounce, so they renamed the soup *leão veloso*. Today the restaurant is owned by a Spanish chef, Ramon Rodriguez, who adapted the recipe to the carioca palate and to the fish available in Rio. He wakes up every day at the crack of dawn to buy fish especially for this soup, which is not only delicious but also lovely to prepare.

SERVES 6–8

FISH STOCK

2 tablespoons olive oil

Head and bones from 1 whole white-fleshed fish (see below)

1 large onion, quartered

2 garlic cloves, peeled

2 stalks celery, cut into 1-inch pieces

3 scallions, white and green parts, cut into 1-inch pieces

5 fresh parsley stems, cut into long pieces

12 cups water

1 whole white-fleshed fish, such as red snapper, branzini, or any other small whole fish, 1½ to 2 pounds, scaled, cleaned, gutted, gills and eyes removed, and filleted (head and bones reserved for the stock)

Kosher salt and freshly ground black pepper

4 tablespoons olive oil

Make the fish stock: In a large Dutch oven, heat the olive oil over medium heat. Add the fish head and bones and cook, turning occasionally, about 4 minutes. Add the onion, garlic, celery, scallions, and parsley stems and cook until the vegetables begin to soften, about 3 minutes. Pour in the water, bring to a boil, then reduce the heat to low and simmer, uncovered, for 1 hour. Skim off any foam that forms. Strain the stock into a large saucepan and keep warm over low heat on the back burner. Discard the solids. (The stock may be prepared up to 3 days ahead of time and kept refrigerated.)

Season the fish fillets with salt and pepper on both sides. Heat 2 tablespoons of the olive oil in a large heavy pot over medium heat. Add the fish and cook until opaque on both sides, about 3 minutes per side. Transfer to a bowl, and when cool enough to handle, finely shred it. Cover with foil and set aside.

In the same pan, add the remaining 2 tablespoons olive oil with the garlic and cook until the garlic is lightly browned, about 3 minutes. Add the onion and bay leaves and cook, stirring frequently, until the onion is softened. Add the tomatoes and cook until they just start to release their liquid, about 3 minutes. Season lightly with salt, pepper, and nutmeg and the paprika and cayenne. Add the wine and bring to a boil; cook until reduced by half. Add the squid and cook, stirring, until opaque, about 2 minutes. Pour in all but 2 cups of the fish stock and bring to a boil.

Meanwhile, add the mussels to the remaining 2 cups stock in the pan. Cover and cook over medium heat, shaking the pan, just until the mussels open, about 3 minutes. Discard any that do not open. Transfer the mussels to the soup.

Season the shrimp with salt and pepper and add to the soup, then add the flaked fish. Simmer over low heat until just cooked through, about 1 minute. Taste and adjust the seasonings. Ladle into warm soup bowls and garnish with the parsley.

3 garlic cloves, finely minced

1 medium onion, finely chopped

2 bay leaves

4 plum tomatoes, peeled, seeded, and chopped

Freshly grated nutmeg

Pinch of paprika

Pinch of cayenne pepper

½ cup dry white wine

1 pound medium squid, cut into ½-inch rings (tentacles left whole)

24 medium mussels, scrubbed

1 pound large shrimp, shelled and deveined

Leaves from 5 sprigs fresh parsley, chopped

COOKING TIP: I find making my own fish stock to be a thing of beauty. Ask your fishmonger to save the fish bones, including a head (eyes and gills removed), for your stock. But if you don't want to go through the trouble of making stock, use prepared fish or shrimp stock and skip to step 2. The stock and vegetables can be prepared ahead of time, but the shellfish should be thrown in just before serving. You can also use other shellfish like lobsters, crab, and scallops. Use the recipe amounts as a guideline, and have fun!

Cabrito Assado do Nova Capela
ROASTED LEG OF LAMB WITH MINT CHIMICHURRI

RESTAURANT: Nova Capela, Av. Mem de Sá, 96 – Centro

My father and I are the lamb lovers in our family. One of our favorite dishes is served at Nova Capela, an old-style, pink-tiled botequim located in Centro. There is nothing epicurean about the way they serve this dish; it comes with a simple side of broccoli, rice and roasted potatoes, but the meat is so tender and velvety that is slides off the bone.

A classic prepared leg of lamb is the kind that roasts for the better part of the day, about 7 hours; at Nova Capela it roasts for 4 hours because they use a younger lamb. It's important to trim some of the fat so that the flavors can infuse the meat but to leave a thin layer of fat to protect the meat from drying out and melt slowly as it roasts. The meat is marinated in garlic, onions, bay leaves, pepper, and wine for 24 hours.

I decided to tackle this lamb recipe in my own kitchen, using American or imported New Zealand lamb, which has a generous layer of fat. Many American markets sell legs of lamb already rolled and tied, but that doesn't give you a chance to season and marinate the meat properly, so I usually undo the roll, flavor it myself, and reroll and tie it again. Feeling a little ambitious, I also prepared a mint chimichurri for this dish

SERVES 6-8

1 bone-in whole leg of lamb, 5 to 6 pounds

Kosher salt and freshly ground black pepper

10 garlic cloves, peeled

4 medium onions, quartered

6 fresh bay leaves

1 cup white wine

1 cup extra virgin olive oil

MINT CHIMICHURRI

1 garlic clove

1 cup fresh mint leaves

¼ cup white wine vinegar

½ cup extra virgin olive oil

1 teaspoon kosher salt

Freshly ground black pepper

Season the lamb generously with salt and pepper all over. Tie the lamb with kitchen twine in 1-inch intervals. Using a paring knife, make 10 deep incisions in the meatiest parts of the lamb, bury the garlic cloves in the incisions, and pinch the meat closed around each clove. Place in a large zip-top bag with the onions, bay leaves, wine, and olive oil, seal the bag, and marinate for 24 hours in the refrigerator. Bring the lamb to room temperature for 1 hour before roasting.

Place a rack in the lower third of the oven and preheat to 450°F.

Place the leg of lamb in a roasting pan and pour the marinade on top; reserve the onion pieces in a bowl. Roast for 30 minutes, then lower the oven temperature to 300°F; continue roasting, basting every hour, until the meat is pulling away from the bone. After the second hour, scatter the onions around the meat and continue roasting. Check the meat with a fork; it should feel like pulled meat after about 4 hours. If not, return the lamb to the oven and continue to cook until it is.

Remove the lamb from the oven and let rest for 20 minutes on a carving board.

While the lamb is resting, make the chimichurri: Place the garlic, mint, and vinegar in a food processor. With the machine running, slowly add the olive oil in a steady stream until well blended. Season with the salt and pepper.

Incorporate the juices from the carving board and roasting pan into the lamb. Carve the lamb from the bone and serve with the chimichurri alongside.

Folheado de Queijo e Presunto
HAM AND CHEESE PUFF PASTRIES

RESTAURANT: Confeitaria Colombo R. Gonçalves Dias, 32 – Centro confeitariacolombo.com.br

Confeitaria Colombo adds a lot of history to Rio's gastronomy. Founded in 1894 at Rua Gonçalves Dias, the bakery displays big mirrors, fancy marble, and interesting tiles. It has offered many different things over the years, but those that remain a constant are the *docinhos* and *salgadinhos*. My own memories of Confeitaria Colombo come from when I worked in Centro and stopped by to eat ham and cheese in puff pastry after work. That was the inspiration for this recipe. Here I kept the approximate size of the *carioca folheado*, but if you want to make these smaller, they make great appetizers or finger food. Many people buy ham and cheese at the deli counter to make sandwiches, so you might already have these ingredients at hand.

You can also substitute turkey and other types of cheese, but my favorite combination is the classic ham and cheese.

MAKES 4

1 package (2 sheets) of store-bought puff pastry, defrosted

All-purpose flour, for rolling

2 tablespoons Dijon mustard

½ pound black forest ham, deli-sliced thin

½ pound deli-sliced cheese (such as Munster, provolone, or mozzarella)

1 egg, lightly beaten for egg wash

Working with one sheet of dough at a time (keep the other one in the fridge), place it on a lightly floured counter and roll out to a 10 x 14-inch rectangle—dust with flour often to prevent the dough from sticking to the surface. Using a pizza cutter, cut the dough into four smaller 7 x 5- inch rectangles. Brush away any excess flour.

Using another dry brush, paint two rectangles with Dijon mustard, leaving a ¾-inch border. Fold 2 to 3 slices of ham, one at a time, and arrange them exactly on top of the mustard. Top with 2 slices of cheese, also folded if necessary. Brush the rectangle borders with egg wash. Carefully place the remaining two pieces of dough on top, lining and pressing the two layers of dough firmly together. Using a fork, pinch the edges to seal tight and use the pizza cutter to trim any excess dough. Repeat the process with the second sheet of puff pastry.

Brush the tops with egg wash and, using a paring knife, cut a small X in the middle to allow steam to come out. Chill the dough for at least 30 minutes or overnight (if you leave overnight, make sure to place them in an airtight plastic container).

Preheat the oven to 375°F.

Arrange all four *folheados* on a sheet pan, leaving at least 2 inches of space between each *folheado,* and bake until puffed, crispy, and golden brown, 20 to 25 minutes, rotating once during baking.

Remove from the oven and transfer to a wire rack. Let cool for a few minutes before serving.

Bife à Milaneza
PANKO-CRUSTED PORK CUTLETS

RESTAURANT: CBar Luiz
ua da Carioca, 39 – Centro
barluiz.com.br

The number of botequims in Rio makes it the shared-plate capital of Brazil. Bar Luíz carries out this concept as classically as I would expect, allowing me to revisit the past in small tidbits whenever I eat there. As a kid, I had no idea that "milaneza" meant a dish prepared in the style of Milan, and I ate *bife à milanesa* quite often in Rio. Today I prefer the dish with pork or veal. This recipe is more of a method then a recipe, and you can use a variety of proteins, such as beef, veal, pork, chicken, or fish. It's the breading that really matters. Manioc flour is what most carioca home cooks will use for the crunchy part, but here I use panko (Japanese breadcrumbs), my favorite choice because it yields the crunchiest and most beautiful coating. You can also use plain breadcrumbs.

SERVES 4

4 thin boneless pork cutlets, about 4 ounces each, pounded very thin

Kosher salt and freshly ground black pepper

½ cup all-purpose flour

2 eggs, lightly beaten

2 cups panko breadcrumbs

1 cup canola oil

Season the meat with salt and pepper on both sides.

Prepare three shallow bowls: one for the flour, seasoned with salt and pepper; one for the eggs, lightly seasoned; and one for the panko.

Just before frying, coat each steak in flour, shaking off the excess, then the eggs, and finally with the panko, pressing the crumbs in well with your hands.

Pour the canola oil into a large skillet; heat over medium heat until it's hot but not smoking. Fry the cutlets two at a time on both sides until the crumbs are golden brown, about 2 minutes per side. Transfer to a plate covered with paper towels. Repeat with the remaining cutlets and serve immediately.

Costelinha de Porco ao Molho de Goiaba

SLOW-ROASTED PORK RIBS WITH GUAVA SAUCE

When I first visited Aconchego Carioca, I knew the chef had to be someone very special. For a long time I wanted to cook with Kátia Barbosa, and on a recent trip to Rio I was invited into her kitchen. On that unforgettable day, she showed me how to prepare this amazing recipe. Kátia likes to use a guava paste with creamy consistency, but if you can only find the firm kind, that's fine; just add a few tablespoons of water to help dissolve it. You can also use quince paste as a substitute.

SERVES 4

2 racks pork spare ribs, about 4 pounds total

Kosher salt and freshly ground black pepper

2 large onions, roughly chopped

6 garlic cloves, crushed

¼ cup olive oil

4 sprigs fresh rosemary or thyme

GUAVA SAUCE

2 tablespoons extra virgin olive oil

4 garlic cloves, crushed and roughly chopped

1 large onion, roughly chopped

2 or 3 bay leaves

2 sprigs of fresh rosemary

½ cup soy sauce

½ cup guava paste

Preheat the oven to 250°F.

Trim any excess fat from the ribs and season with salt and pepper on both sides. Place the rib racks in a large roasting pan, lay the onions and garlic on and around the racks, and drizzle with the olive oil. Roast for 4 hours; the first hour uncovered, then add the herbs, cover tightly with foil, and roast for another 3 hours, checking and basting hourly. You can roast the ribs up to 3 days ahead, cool them, and keep them wrapped in plastic in the refrigerator.

Make the guava sauce: In a medium saucepan, heat the olive oil over low heat. Add the garlic and cook until it just starts to turn golden. Add the onion, bay leaves, and rosemary and cook until the onion is softened and translucent, about 4 minutes.

Add the soy sauce and bring to a boil. Add the guava paste and mix well until dissolved. Simmer the sauce until slightly thickened, 5 to 7 minutes. Remove the bay leaves and rosemary, transfer the sauce to a food processor, and process until smooth. Return the sauce to the pan.

When the pork ribs have roasted for 4 hours, brush with a heavy coating of the guava sauce (use all of the sauce) and return the ribs to the oven for another 30 minutes, turning every 10 minutes and brushing with sauce after each turn, until the ribs have a rich glaze. Remove the ribs from the oven and cut into 1- or 2-rib portions. (Alternately, if the ribs were cooked ahead of time, cut them into small portions and reheat with the sauce, adding a few drops of water if necessary.)

RESTAURANT: Aconchego Carioca, Rua Barao de Iguatemi, 379 Praça da Bandeira aconchegocarioca.com.br

Pastel de Angú
POLENTA TURNOVER

Regular cornmeal will not work for this recipe; you need to use superfine cornmeal (*farinha de fubá*), preferably the Brazilian brand Yoki. I recommend using thin rubber gloves when kneading the dough as it's hot and sticky.

MAKES 15

1¾ cups water

1 teaspoon kosher salt, plus more for seasoning

1¼ cups superfine cornmeal (*farinha de fubá*)

½ cup Catupiry cheese

2 tablespoons dried oregano

Freshly ground black pepper

2½ cups vegetable oil

Pour the water into a saucepan, add the salt, and bring to a boil.

Slowly sprinkle in the cornmeal, whisking constantly until blended. Switch to a wooden spoon and stir, working on and off the heat, until the cornmeal gathers like dough. Touch it—don't worry, the dough won't burn you—it should have the consistency of modeling clay. If the mixture feels dry, add up to 2 tablespoons of water at a time until it forms a cohesive dough.

Turn the dough out onto a large wooden cutting board. Cool for 1 minute, then while still hot, wear gloves and knead the dough well and into a ball. Cut in half and cover each half with plastic wrap.

In a small bowl, mix the cheese with the oregano. Season with salt and pepper.

Have a small bowl of water and a pastry brush nearby. Working with half the dough at a time, press the dough down and roll it out to ¼ inch thick. Using a 3-inch round cookie cutter, cut out circles of dough and cover them with a sheet of plastic so they don't dry out. Working with one dough circle at a time, hold a circle in your palm and press with your thumb gently, curving the circle upward. Spoon a teaspoon of the filling into the center of the circle, brush the edges lightly with water, and fold it in half. Using your fingers, tightly pinch the edges together to seal. This is the tricky part, because as you fold, the center has a tendency to crack. Patch the dough in the center if that happens, making sure there are no leaks, though a very light crack on the sides is okay. Don't worry if the half moon shape doesn't look perfect; it's more important to patch the dough. Arrange the filled turnovers on a baking sheet and cover loosely with plastic wrap. Repeat with the remaining dough circles and filling. (The filled turnovers can be covered and refrigerated for up to 2 hours before cooking, or frozen for up to 6 months; freeze in a single layer on a parchment paper-lined tray, then transfer to freezer bags.)

Pour the vegetable oil into a heavy-bottomed pot and heat to 350°F, as measured by a deep-fat thermometer. Fry the turnovers in batches, adding as many as will fit without touching each other. Turn them occasionally with a long slotted spoon for 4 minutes—they will not take on a lot of color, just darken slightly (don't cook much longer or the cheese could pop out). Transfer to a plate covered with paper towels. Continue working in batches until all the turnovers are fried. Serve with the pork ribs (page 122).

Pudim de Claras com Baba de Moça
EGG WHITE PUDDING WITH COCONUT CREAM SAUCE

RESTAURANT: O Navegador, Av. Rio Branco, 180/6 andar, Clube Naval, onavegador.com.br

When I lived in Rio, I worked in an investment bank located in Centro. We had business lunches at O Navegador, and I always swooned over the *pudim de claras*. Traditionally it's served with the coconut cream sauce that I'm including here, but you can also serve it with berries or a berry sauce. After all this time, the restaurant is more alive than ever, and its chef (for the past thirty years), Tereza Corção, is gaining recognition for her work. She is one of the leaders of carioca new gastronomy, combining elaborate technique with local ingredients.

SERVES 6–8

2 cups sugar

4 tablespoons water

6 large egg whites, at room temperature

⅛ teaspoon salt

1 teaspoon vanilla extract

½ teaspoon fresh lime juice

COCONUT CREAM SAUCE

9 tablespoons unsalted butter

½ cup sugar

½ cup coconut milk (preferably a Brazilian brand like Sococo)

8 large egg yolks

SPECIAL EQUIPMENT:
One 8-cup tube mold

Combine 1 cup of the sugar and the water in a very clean heavy-bottomed saucepan. Cook over high heat without stirring until it forms a light amber-colored caramel, about 5 minutes. Pour the caramel into the tube mold and swirl it around, making sure the caramel evenly covers the whole bottom of the pan. Set aside.

Preheat the oven to 250°F.

Place the egg whites in the bowl of an electric mixer (make sure it's spotlessly clean) fitted with the whisk attachment. Start beating at medium speed until the eggs start foaming, rising, and turning opaque. Gradually add the remaining 1 cup sugar, dissolving it into the egg whites. Increase the speed to high and beat until the meringue is firm and glossy, 5 to 8 minutes.

Add the vanilla and lime juice. Carefully transfer the meringue to the mold using a spatula to spread evenly inside the mold. Place the tube pan in a roasting pan. Pour hot water into the roasting pan to come halfway up the sides of the pan. Carefully transfer to the oven and bake until the top is very lightly browned, about 1 hour and 15 minutes.

Meanwhile, make the coconut cream sauce: In a medium saucepan, combine the butter, sugar, and coconut milk. Place over medium heat and cook until the sugar dissolves, the butter melts, and the mixture starts to bubble slightly.

In a medium bowl, beat the egg yolks.

Slowly pour half of the hot coconut mixture over the yolks, whisking as you pour, to temper the yolks. Return everything to the saucepan and cook over low heat, stirring constantly, until it thickens to a curd consistency, 10 to 15 minutes.

Strain through a fine sieve into a medium bowl and let cool to room temperature. (You can prepare the sauce up to 3 days ahead of time and keep in a tightly sealed container in the refrigerator.)

Turn the oven off, open the oven door, and keep the tube and roasting pan inside the oven for another 10 minutes to prevent a shock of temperature. Transfer the tube pan to a cooling rack and cool completely. Run a knife around the mold and invert onto a cake platter. Let the caramel drip for a few minutes, then lift the tube pan off. Serve cold or at room temperature, with the coconut cream sauce on the side. To store, cover loosely with plastic wrap in the fridge for up to 2 days.

Pudim de Tapioca

TAPIOCA PUDDING WITH COCONUT CARAMEL SAUCE

This dessert came to Rio from the kitchens of Rodrigo Oliveira, an extremely talented chef based in São Paulo. Like many other desserts, it didn't take too long to spread across Rio. I got inspired to try it when visiting Feira São Cristovão, a flea market in Centro specializing in foods from the northeast region of Brazil. As a carioca, I love all kinds of pudding, and I especially love the humble tapioca, which offers an irresistibly fluffy and chewy consistency. Rodrigo serves this dessert with a coconut caramel sauce and toasted coconut. These are great complements to the pudding, but even served plain it still tastes amazing.

SERVES 8

½ cup granulated tapioca
  (or small pearl tapioca)

1½ cups heavy cream

¾ cup plus 2 tablespoons
  coconut milk

1 cup sugar

⅓ cup water

2 large eggs

2 large egg yolks

½ cup whole milk

One 14-ounce can sweetened
  condensed milk

1 teaspoon vanilla extract

COCONUT CARAMEL SAUCE

2 cups granulated sugar

¾ cup plus 2 tablespoons
  coconut milk

⅓ cup water

4 ounces unsweetened
  grated coconut

SPECIAL EQUIPMENT:
One 8-cup tube mold

Place the tapioca in a medium bowl and pour the heavy cream and coconut milk over it. Cover with plastic wrap and let sit for 2 hours at room temperature or overnight in the refrigerator.

Combine the sugar and water in a clean heavy-bottomed saucepan and cook over high heat without stirring until it turns into an amber-colored caramel, about 5 minutes. Pour the caramel into the tube mold, making sure it coats the whole bottom of the pan evenly.

Preheat the oven to 350°F.

In a large bowl, beat the eggs, yolks, milk, sweetened condensed milk, and vanilla. Strain through a sieve into the tapioca and mix gently with a rubber spatula. Carefully pour into the prepared caramel pan. Transfer to a large roasting pan and fill the pan with hot tap water to come halfway up the sides of the pan. Transfer the roasting pan to the center of the oven and bake until the pudding is thick but still wobbles in the center, 45 to 55 minutes.

Meanwhile, make the coconut caramel sauce: Place the sugar in a medium saucepan and cook over high heat until it turns amber in color. Add the coconut milk and water and cook until it thickens, about 5 minutes.

Spread the grated coconut onto a baking sheet and bake until lightly browned, turning constantly, about 4 minutes.

Transfer the custard mold to a wire rack and cool to room temperature, then refrigerate for at least 4 hours or overnight. It's important to invert the pudding only after it is chilled completely, otherwise it might break.

When ready to serve, run a smooth knife around the inside of the tube pan. Place a large rimmed serving platter on top of the pan, and holding it together with both hands, quickly invert the pudding onto the platter. Allow the caramel to run down before lifting up the tube mold. Drizzle some of the coconut caramel sauce around it and garnish with the toasted coconut.

BARRA DA TIJUCA

BARRA: THE FUTURE

As a child growing up in Rio, I saw Barra da Tijuca go from deserted to one of the most developed neighborhoods in town.

To enter Barra, you have to drive through Rocinha, the largest *favela* (shanty town) of Brazil. I grew up just a few minutes away, but I never connected with this world—so close to my own home yet so far away from the world I grew up in. Until the day I decided to visit, when my whole perspective of Rio changed.

I expected that our societies would have nothing to do with each other, but in Rio links between different people are made every day, at every moment, through sun and landscape, music and sports, but most important, through food. Food can be a class divider, but in Rio it is a class connector, a common ground, an equalizer—through flavor.

The same *feijoada* (page 38) that is served at gorgeous hotels is also served in Rocinha. The same *bolinho de bacalhau* (cod fritters, page 20) that are served in the cool botequims in the trendy neighborhoods of Ipanema and Leblon are also served here as well, on the way to Barra, or in any other *favela* in Rio.

Two worlds facing each other: look to the right and you'll see the most magnificent view of Rio; look to the left and you'll see Rocinha, also magnificent in its own way.

Barra is the future. The neighborhood is being transformed to host the 2016 Olympic Games to become the home of the Olympic village. Nearly half of the sports competitions will take place at Barra, where construction of a new street called Rua Carioca Entertainment Boulevard and a private Olympic beach exclusive for the athletes are in the works.

Today this road to improvement, with more than thirty shopping malls, countless *churrascarias* (steakhouses), and many botequims, is just four years away, and that's our reality. High, low, rich, poor, Rio's geographical structure, its gorgeous sunny climate—and the food—bring our population together, always outdoors and beyond the social patterns that separate most cities' populations by class, race, or occupation.

The difference between now and when I grew up in Rio is that the culture that springs from neighborhoods traditionally marginalized by society is now being integrated with the rest of the city, and cariocas of all classes go to the *favelas* not just as tourists but to participate in our homegrown culture, trying local dishes, bars, and dance spots. I left Rocinha *favela* feeling hopeful for the future and proud of being a carioca.

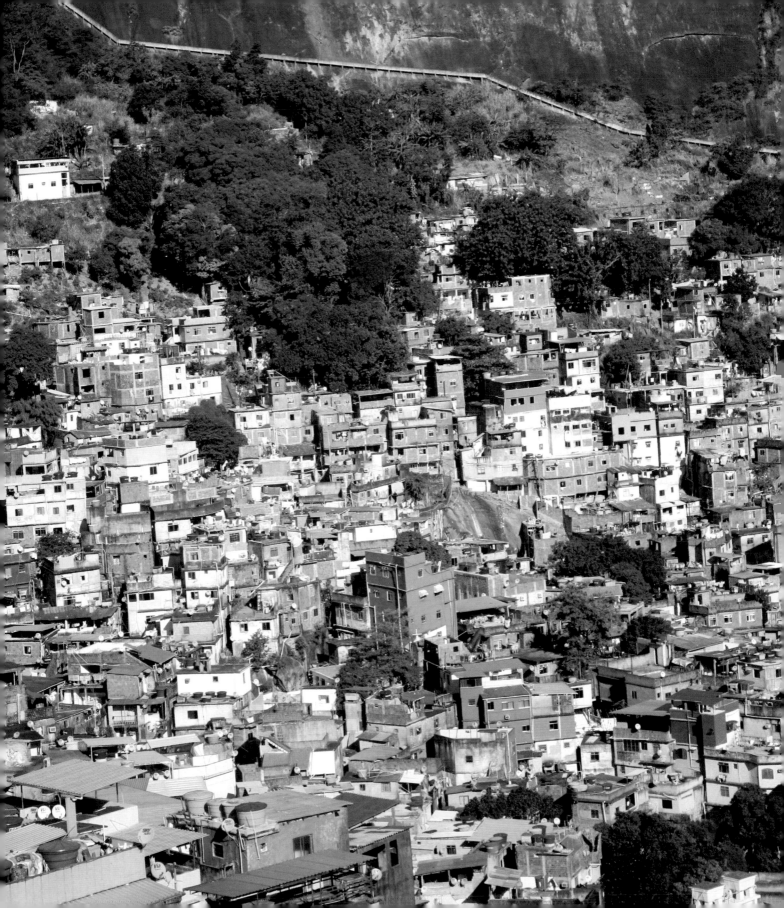

Suco de Frutas Vermelhas
RED BERRY FRUIT JUICE

RESTAURANT: Big Polis
Av. Ataulfo de Paiva, 505 –
Rio de Janeiro

Each beach in Rio is a world unto itself; Barra's beaches stretch further than other neighborhoods', with many juice bars right across from the beach. Big Polis is a classic chain in Rio with branches all over town, including one in Barra. One of my favorite juices at Big Polis is the *suco de frutas vermelhas,* which is prepared with red fruits such as strawberries, raspberries, blackberries, and açaí. When I moved to the United States, I found very little to satisfy my craving, so I make my own juice every day of the week using cherries, blueberries, or blackberries. Like mother, like daughter, mine is as addicted to these healthy concoctions as I am, and she likes to prepare this particular one for breakfast every morning.

SERVES 1

3 large strawberries

⅓ cup raspberries

⅓ cup blueberries or cherries
or blackberries

1 cup water

3 tablespoons sugar

Combine all the ingredients in a blender and blend until very smooth, about 3 minutes.

Strain over a tall glass and serve immediately.

Aipim Frito
YUCCA FRIES

I love yucca. I call it the miracle vegetable of Brazil, because it has been providing food for generations of native Brazilians, Africans, and Portuguese and is used in an infinite number of recipes in many forms, including starches, flours, and juices. This vegetable is also widely available in American supermarkets and is very easy to prepare. Depending on the quality of the yucca, boiling and frying times might vary. In Rio *aipim frito* is often served as a side dish by itself. You can also serve it as a snack with a spicy mayonnaise sauce made by flavoring mayonnaise with minced garlic, chopped cilantro and parsley, lime juice, and salt and pepper.

SERVES 4–6

2 pounds fresh yucca
  (about 2)

Kosher salt

3 cups vegetable oil

Peel the yucca and cut it into 2½-inch sections. Wash well to remove any dirt, and cut it into ⅓-inch-thick sticks.

Place the yucca in a large pot and add cold water to cover completely. Add a good pinch of salt and bring to a boil over high heat. Reduce the heat to medium-low and cook gently until almost translucent and a knife inserted comes out easily, about 20 minutes. Using a slotted spoon, transfer to a baking sheet covered with paper towels, spreading the yucca in one layer. Let dry and cool to room temperature. Using a paring knife, remove the woody fibers from the yucca.

Pour the vegetable oil into a heavy-bottomed pot and heat it to 350°F, as measured by a deep-fat thermometer. Working in batches, slip the yucca into the oil, turning occasionally, until light golden brown, 5 to 7 minutes per batch. Remove with a slotted spoon and place on a baking sheet lined with paper towels; season with salt immediately as the fries come out of the oil.

INGREDIENT NOTE: This tuber vegetable goes by many different names: yucca, cassava, manioc, and in Portuguese *aipim, mandioca, macaxeira*. I know of no other vegetable with that many names. For the sake of consistency, let's call it yucca in English and *aipim* in Portuguese. Yucca has a woody fiber in the center, and the older the yucca gets, the tougher this fiber is. You can remove it before boiling or afterward (which I find is easier, as you'll see in the recipe).

Sanduiche Natural de Galinha com Cenoura

CHICKEN SALAD WITH CARROTS AND CHIVES ON WHOLE WHEAT

This sandwich is a benchmark of Rio's beaches, and I grew up eating it. We'll never know which beach vendor started selling these by yelling "*Oooooolha o sanduiche natural!*" (Look! It's the natural sandwich!), but it certainly was a good marketing strategy. The word natural must have come from using whole wheat bread instead of white bread, but what really matters is that these sandwiches are delicious! It's a sandwich that lives inside of me, a sandwich that connects me with Rio every time I sit down to lunch on one.

You can roast the chicken or use store-bought rotisserie chicken, and make sure to use shredded chicken rather than cubed chicken to give the sandwich the right texture. Herbs aren't traditionally used in Rio, but I like how chives complement the flavors of the sandwich (parsley works too), so I include them in mine. In Rio the sandwich is served ready-made and wrapped in plastic. As it sits, the juicy mixture and all its tasty flavors permeate the bread in a soggy, blissful way, making it a perfect sandwich to pack and go.

MAKES 4

3 tablespoons dark or golden raisins

2 medium carrots

1½ cups finely shredded chicken

½ cup mayonnaise

2 tablespoons chopped fresh chives

Kosher salt and freshly ground black pepper

8 slices whole wheat bread

Plump the raisins by soaking them in ½ cup warm water for 5 minutes.

Meanwhile, grate the carrots on the largest holes of a box grater; you should have about 1 cup grated carrots. Place the carrots in a bowl.

Drain the raisins and add them to the bowl with the chicken, mayonnaise, and chives. Season with salt and pepper and mix the ingredients with a rubber spatula.

Divide the mixture among the bread slices and sandwich them together.

Bacalhau à Lagareira

FRESH COD WITH ONIONS, GARLIC, POTATOES, AND BROCCOLINI

RESTAURANT: Adegão Português, R. Shopping Rio Design Barra, Av das Americas, 7.777, 3° piso, Barra da Tijuca, adegaoportugues.com.br

Lagareiro is the Portuguese word for a person who owns an olive oil press, and indeed, olive oil is an important ingredient in this recipe. This recipe is incredibly simple, yet it delivers flavors in a brilliant way. At the restaurant Adegão Português, the recipe is prepared using salt cod, but here I make it with fresh cod since it is widely available in the United States. Every time I make this dish, without fail I am asked for the recipe. It is healthy and very easy to put together—everything can be prepared ahead of time and refrigerated for up to 2 days, with the dish assembled just before baking.

SERVES 4

1½ pounds small new potatoes

Kosher salt

1 pound broccolini, thick lower stems removed

6 tablespoons extra virgin olive oil

2 medium onions, thinly sliced

4 garlic cloves, minced

1¼ pounds fresh cod, cut into 4 equal pieces

¼ cup white wine, water, or fish stock

Freshly ground black pepper

Place the potatoes in a large heavy saucepan and cover with cold water by at least 1 inch. Add a large pinch of salt and bring to a boil. Reduce the heat to medium and simmer until the potatoes are fork-tender, 12 to 15 minutes. Drain in a colander and spread onto a plate. When cool enough to handle, peel and quarter the potatoes. Set aside in a bowl.

Preheat the oven to 350°F. Lightly coat a large shallow baking dish with cooking spray.

Place the broccolini in a steamer or a pot fitted with a steaming basket over simmering water. Season with salt, cover the pot, and steam until the stalks are just tender, about 5 minutes. Transfer the broccolini to a plate and set aside.

Heat 2 tablespoons of the olive oil in a large skillet over low heat, add the onions, and cook, stirring occasionally with a wooden spoon, until softened and translucent, about 10 minutes. (Resist the temptation to turn the heat to high, or the onions will brown; the slower you cook the onions, the sweeter they get.) Transfer to the bowl with potatoes and toss together; season lightly with salt and pepper.

In a small skillet, heat 1 tablespoon of the remaining olive oil over low heat and add the garlic. Cook until it just starts to turn golden, 1 to 2 minutes. Immediately transfer to a plate lined with double thickness of paper towels.

Arrange the potato-onion mixture on the bottom of the baking dish and place the broccolini on top.

Season the cod with salt and pepper and arrange on top of the vegetables. Sprinkle the garlic on top, drizzle the remaining 3 tablespoons olive oil all over, and bake until the fish is just cooked, 12 to 15 minutes.

Remove the baking dish from the oven; spoon the cod onto warm plates and serve immediately.

Purê de Abóbora com Carne Seca
PULLED CARNE SECA WITH BUTTERNUT SQUASH PUREE

RESTAURANT: Devassa, Rua Sen Vergueiro 2, Rio de Janeiro
devassa.com.br

Carne seca, a dried and salt-cured meat, is a huge part of Brazilian cooking. It comes from a lean cut such as top round, because too much marbled fat (what gives that buttery richness we want in our cooked meats) makes the dried meat too tough. This dish is a botequim-inspired delicacy, like one I've had at Devassa, a botequim in Barra.

SERVES 6

2¼ pounds *carne seca*

3 tablespoons extra virgin olive oil

2 large onions, thinly sliced

Kosher salt and freshly ground black pepper

¼ cup chopped fresh parsley

2 tablespoons olive oil

1 medium butternut squash, peeled, seeded, and diced

Pinch of freshly grated nutmeg

Pinch of cinnamon

Pinch of sugar

2 tablespoons unsalted butter

COOKING TIP: This recipe calls for advance planning, as it requires reconstituting the meat by soaking it in cold water overnight. Brazilians like to use a pressure cooker for everything, so we often use one for carne seca to make it tender, but braising is a perfect alternative. This can be done up to two days ahead of time; keep the meat in the braising liquid. If you cannot find carne seca, substitute a strong-flavored smoked meat or brisket. As long as you use some sort of pulled meat that's full of flavor, this dish will taste delicious.

Rinse the carne seca in cold water and place it inside a large container. Cover with cold water, cover the container, and store in the refrigerator for 12 to 24 hours, changing the water at least 3 times.

Place the meat in a saucepan, fill with water to cover halfway, cover the pot, bring to a simmer, and cook over low heat for at least 3 hours, until the meat is tender. Alternatively, cook in a pressure cooker for 45 minutes after the pressure starts.

Remove the meat from the pan and discard the water. When the meat is cool enough to handle, thinly shred it, discarding the fat and any undesired grisly parts. You should have about 2 cups meat.

In a large skillet, heat the extra virgin olive oil over medium heat and add the onions. Cook, stirring frequently with a wooden spoon, until softened, about 10 minutes. If the onions start to get some color, add 1 to 2 tablespoons water. Add the pulled meat, season with pepper, and sprinkle with the parsley.

In a medium saucepan, heat the regular olive oil over medium heat. Add the butternut squash and cook, stirring frequently with a wooden spoon, for 5 minutes. Partially cover the pan and cook until the squash is tender, checking frequently to make sure it doesn't brown (if it does, add about ¼ cup water), 15 to 20 minutes. Season with salt and pepper and add the nutmeg, cinnamon, and sugar. Add the butter and stir well.

Transfer to a food processor and puree the pumpkin until smooth.

Arrange the puree on an oval platter, spoon the pulled meat mixture on top, and serve immediately.

BÚZIOS

A TRIP TO BÚZIOS

Búzios is one of Brazil's best beach resorts, and a mere three hours from Rio by car. The map of Búzios is a peninsula clipped with many small bays (over twenty), each one hosting a breathtaking beach.

main attraction in town, and the boardwalk was named Orla Bardot in her honor.

The reason Búzios is so appealing to me is not only because of its heavenly beaches, but because of its ability to keep nature intact. The paths to the shore remain so unmarked by modernity that you feel as though you've strayed back a century in time with the dusty roads and improvised trails.

With it, comes another aspect that I love about Búzios: the lack of foreign influence in its food. In Búzios you can truly eat like a fisherman. No matter what beach you stay in, *comida típica Buziana* (typical food from Búzios) is served. Grilled fish, salads, sandwiches, and lots of different juices are just a few of the delicious foods of Búzios.

They are the inspiration for the recipes in this chapter, like farfalle with salmon and caipirinha (inspired by a fish market; page 146), a seven fruit salad (inspired by Geribá beach; page 149), while others are inspired by the effervescent night life of Búzios like the *crepe dos reis* (from Chez Michou; page 145).

Originally settled by European smugglers of Pau Brazil wood and slave traders during the 17th century, this region prospered and became a picturesque fishing village. It was only in the 1960s, however, that the region found more notoriety after Brigitte Bardot, the famous French actress, fell in love with Búzios and made it her second home. Her statue is now a

Suco de Abacaxi com Hortelã
PINEAPPLE AND MINT SMOOTHIE

This simple smoothie is good for you, but that's not the only reason to give it a try. It is also a delicious little piece of Rio, where pineapples are sweet as honey, that you can make at home in seconds for an instant pick-me-up. It doesn't require any exotic ingredients or techniques, and the combination of pineapple and mint packs this smoothie with a blast of brightness. Pick a fruit that feels heavy for its size, has a fresh fragrance, and gives slightly when pressed at the base. The vendors at the market in Rio tap on the pineapples, searching for the sound of ripeness, like a full drum compared to a hollow one, and that's how I pick my pineapples too.

SERVES 1

2 cups cubed pineapple (about ½ pineapple)

⅓ cup mint leaves

1 to 2 tablespoons sugar, to taste

½ cup water, plus more if needed

Place the pineapple, mint leaves, and sugar in a blender. Add the water and blend until smooth. Serve in a highball glass over ice.

Crepe Chez Michouz
BRIE AND APRICOT CRÊPES

Chez Michou opened in 1983, when Búzios offered very little in terms of gastronomy, by two Argentineans and three Belgians who were looking to make Búzios their hometown. Located on the trendy Rua das Pedras, it's easier to get a table a Chez Michou during the day, but if you want to understand what Búzios is all about, go at night and you'll see one of the most buzzed-about places on earth, especially during Christmas and New Year's. Sometimes the crowd is so big you can't even get close to the restaurant. But that's the charm of Rua das Pedras: it's a place to see and be seen.

When I was a young adult still living in Rio, we would go to Chez Michou to try to find the men of our dreams, but instead I found the crêpes of my dreams. Their crêpes come in a variety of flavors, both savory and sweet. One of my favorites is *crepe dos reis* (king's crêpe) with the classic combination of Brie and jam. It's light and refreshing yet satisfying and indulgent.

MAKES 10

2 large eggs

1 cup whole milk

⅛ teaspoon salt

1½ tablespoons sugar

1 tablespoon unsalted butter, melted, plus more for cooking

½ cup all-purpose flour

½ cup apricot jam

8 ounces Brie cheese, at room temperature, cut into ¼-inch-thick slices, then cut into 1-inch pieces

Confectioners' sugar for dusting

Place the eggs, milk, salt, and sugar in a food processor or blender and process until smooth. Add the butter and process until combined. Add the flour and process until just incorporated. The flour should be completely blended, but don't overprocess.

Pour the batter into a large measuring cup or a large plastic container, cover, and chill for at least 1 hour. The batter will thicken as it chills, but it should pour easily (if it's too thick, add a few drops of milk).

Whisk the batter if any foam formed on top. Heat a small nonstick skillet over medium heat. Drop a pinch of butter the size of a pea into the pan and swirl it around. Working fast, pour 2 to 3 tablespoons of batter in the pan, just to thinly coat the bottom. Cook until the bottom is golden, about 2 minutes (take a peek using an offset spatula). Flip it over and cook the other side for about 1 minute. (The second side never looks as handsome as the first side, coming out with dark spots.)

Transfer to a cutting board (nice side facing down) and spread a thin layer of apricot jam on top. Add 2 or 3 pieces of Brie and fold the crepe in half. (If you prefer, fold the crêpe in quarters.) Repeat with the remaining batter and crêpes. (You can prepare the crêpes ahead of time and keep them stacked and wrapped in the refrigerator; to reheat, wrap the stack in foil and bake in a preheated 350°F oven for 5 minutes.) Sprinkle with confectioners' sugar and serve warm.

RESTAURANT: Chez Michou Crêperie, Av. José Bento Ribeiro Dantas, 90 Armação dos Búzios – Búzios, chezmichou.com.br

COOKING TIPS: As with any crêpe, the batter is quite simple to make and can be prepared up to 2 days ahead of time, kept in the refrigerator. I don't mind the rind on the Brie, but if you don't like it, go ahead and remove it.

Farfalle com Salmon ao Molho de Caipirinha
FARFALLE WITH SALMON AND CAIPIRINHA SAUCE

Búzios is known for its famous beaches, but also for its *pescadores*, or fishermen, true heroes who provide many fish markets in Rio with fresh fish. A trip to the fish market in Búzios makes my head spin. At the crack of dawn the market displays rows and rows of white plastic bins filled with ice and about fifty pounds worth of whole fish in each—red snapper, tuna, salmon, lobsters, octopus, and many more—that had been unloaded from boats just a few hours earlier. They also sell directly to the customer, so the last time I was there, before going back to Rio I bought a piece of salmon (and lots of ice for the three-hour car drive) and used it to create this easy and elegant dish rooted in carioca groove. Here is how it works: You roast the salmon and flake it. Make a sauce based on shallots, add stock (it can be fish, chicken, or pasta water), and then, *ta-da*, you throw in the flavors of a caipirinha: cachaça, lime zest, and lime juice, so the pasta and fish get drunk in caipirinha flavors, just like a carioca.

SERVES 4

12 ounces salmon, skin on

Kosher salt and freshly ground
  black pepper

10 ounces farfalle pasta

2 tablespoons extra virgin
  olive oil

1 large shallot, finely
  chopped

2 cups chicken stock

1 cup heavy cream

⅓ cup cachaça

Finely grated zest of 1 lime

2 tablespoons fresh lime juice

¼ cup chopped fresh
  cilantro

Preheat the oven to 350°F.

Season the salmon with salt and pepper on both sides, place on a greased baking sheet, and roast until almost cooked through, 6 to 8 minutes. Remove from the oven and let cool slightly, then flake the fish into big chunks. (You should have about 2 cups.) Keep covered.

Bring a large pot of water to a boil over high heat and add a good pinch of salt. Add the pasta and cook according to the package instructions to al dente. Drain, saving some of the cooking liquid, and transfer the pasta to a bowl.

Meanwhile, heat the olive oil in a large skillet over medium heat. Add the shallot and cook, stirring occasionally, until softened but not browned, about 4 minutes. Add the chicken stock, bring to boil, and cook until it just starts to reduce, about 3 minutes. Add the cream, reduce the heat to low, and cook until it starts to thicken, about 5 minutes. Season lightly with salt and pepper.

Remove from the heat and stir in the cachaça, lime zest, and lime juice. Add the pasta and salmon and heat over low heat, tossing with tongs, until the fish is just heated through. Add the cilantro and toss. Taste and adjust the seasonings if needed. If the dish needs a bit more liquid, add some of the reserved pasta water.

Sanduiche de Atum
TUNA SANDWICH

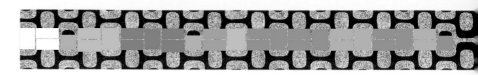

Growing up in Rio, there were three classic cold sandwiches a carioca would eat for lunch: egg salad sandwich, chicken salad sandwich (see page 135), and tuna salad sandwich. I was almost twenty-five before I realized that this trio of sandwiches existed in other countries. This recipe is inspired by a sandwich I ate at Sukão in Búzios that uses tomatoes (I use cherry tomatoes), lettuce (I substituted arugula), and whole wheat bread (but feel free to use any type).

MAKES 4

Two 5-ounce cans tuna, preferably packed in olive oil, drained and flaked

1 tablespoon finely chopped shallots

½ stalk celery, finely diced

3 tablespoons coarsely chopped black olives

¼ cup mayonnaise

A few drops of fresh lime juice

2 tablespoons chopped fresh dill

Kosher salt and freshly ground black pepper

8 slices whole wheat bread

4 ounces (about 12) cherry tomatoes, quartered

3 ounces arugula

RESTAURANT: Sukão Bar, Praca Eugenio Honold, Barrio Ossos – Buzios

In a large bowl, combine the tuna, shallots, celery, olives, mayonnaise, lime juice, and dill. Season with salt and pepper and mix well. Cover and refrigerate for at least 1 hour for the flavors to develop.

Lightly toast the bread.

Fold the tomatoes into the tuna mixture, divide the mixture among the bread slices, top with arugula, and sandwich them together.

Salada de Frutas
SEVEN FRUIT SALAD WITH COCONUT FLAKES AND FRESH MINT

Salada de frutas is another staple of carioca cuisine and is standard beach food. This recipe is inspired by a version I tried in Búzios and can be made with a variety of fruits. Use this recipe as a guideline; any melon, citrus, or stone fruit can be added. I like to add honey because it dissolves nicely into the orange juice, but an equal amount of table sugar will work as well. Once the orange juice is mixed and the salad sits, the fruit starts losing its bright color and shape, so pour the juice just before serving. This fruit salad is served for dessert; if you want to jazz it up, finish it with a dollop of whipped cream or a scoop of vanilla ice cream.

SERVES 4–6

1 cup dried coconut flakes

¾ cup orange juice

2 tablespoons honey

1 cup diced pineapple
(about ¼ pineapple)

1 cup diced mango
(about 1 mango)

1 cup raspberries

1 cup hulled and quartered
strawberries (about 6)

1 cup halved seedless
red grapes

1 cup diced ripe papaya
(about 1)

1¼ cups diced banana
(about 2)

1 teaspoon finely grated
lime zest

2 tablespoons chopped
fresh mint

Preheat the oven to 300°F.

Spread the coconut on a small baking sheet and toast in the oven until it is very lightly browned, rotating the sheet once, about 4 minutes. Transfer to a bowl and set aside.

In a small bowl, whisk the orange juice and honey.

In a large bowl, combine all the fruit and gently mix with a spatula. Pour in the orange juice-honey mixture and add the lime zest and mint. Fold carefully to coat the fruit.

Pour into serving bowls, garnish with the toasted coconut, and serve immediately.

BARCO≈GANDHY≈
ALUGA-SE≈PASSEIO≈
E PESCA.
LOTAÇÃO≈ 14+1
TEL (CEL) 88112348
CAPITANIA TEL 33711583

PARATY

PARATY: A COASTAL TOWN

Paraty is located on the coast between Rio de Janeiro and São Paulo; it was founded in 1667. The soil around the region is perfect for sugarcane plantations, and since the old days the region has been cluttered with mills producing cachaça. During the seventeeth and eighteenth centuries, a triangular path linking Rio de Janeiro to Minas Gerais and São Paulo known as *Caminho do Ouro* (the gold path) brought even more prosperity to Paraty, as its harbors strategically served as a place to ship gold to Portugal.

The histories of cachaça and Paraty are intertwined on cultural, economic, and social levels. The city consists of a harbor crowded with tourist boats, four churches, and the historic center, in which you'll find charming boutiques selling crafts and cachaça from the mills of the region, which are more active now than ever. As a caipirinha devotee, I got lost in a store called Armazém da Cachaça, which sells hundreds of cachaças of every taste: sweet, salty, spicy, blended, aged in carvalho wood and jequitibá. Just a few blocks away, another store, Espaço da Cachaça, offered the same kind of experience. This cachaça bonanza inspired the delicious caipi-coco cake, on page 158.

Other recipes in this chapter are inspired by a visit to a typical Paraty restaurant called Banana da Terra, where you'll find plenty of fish dishes but it was their *bolinha de queijo* (page 155) that made me swoon, and the fish boats of Paraty, where I bought shrimp for the roasted garlic-ginger recipe on page 157.

Batida de Côco
COCONUT COCKTAIL

Batida de côco is a classic cocktail served at all the bars in Rio, and this version is inspired by the many cachaçarias around Paraty. A vendor at the store Armazém da Cachaça told me that he likes to mix vodka and cachaça, which is what I do here. The cocktail is lighter using this combination, though you can use only cachaça if you prefer. I generally like my cocktails on the lighter side, but you can feel free to use a stronger dose of either or both of the liquors than what I suggest here.

SERVES 6

¾ cup coconut milk

One 14-ounce can sweetened condensed milk

1 cup vodka

¼ cup cachaça

½ cup unsweetened grated coconut

Combine all the ingredients in a blender and blend until smooth. Pour into an ice-filled glass and serve.

Bolinha de Queijo
CHEESE FRITTERS

RESTAURANT: Bannana Da Terra
Rua Dr Samuel Costa 198 – Paraty
restaurantebananadaterra.com.br

This recipe is based on a snack that is served at Banana Da Terra, a restaurant in Paraty. These crisp little nuggets of cheese dough provide a wonderful crunch and then melt in your mouth. You can't eat just one. *Bolinha de queijo* is a classic botequim food from the 1980s that disappeared from restaurant menus for a while but is increasingly, and with good reason, showing up all over Rio again. Ana Bueno, the chef behind this lovely restaurant, likes to serve these with a dollop of plantain puree stuffed inside, but I skipped that step in the interest of keeping things simple.

MAKES ABOUT 50

½ cup (1 stick) unsalted butter

3 tablespoons extra virgin olive oil

⅓ cup finely minced shallot

Kosher salt and freshly ground black pepper

¾ cup cornstarch

2 cups whole milk

1⅓ cups all-purpose flour

Pinch of cayenne

Freshly grated nutmeg

½ cup finely grated Parmesan cheese

8 ounces Provolone cheese, cut into ¾-inch cubes

2½ cups vegetable oil for frying

1 large egg, lightly whisked

1 cup breadcrumbs

In a medium saucepan, melt the butter in the olive oil over low heat. Add the shallot and cook until softened, about 3 minutes. Season lightly with salt and pepper.

In a small bowl, whisk the cornstarch with the milk. Pour the mixture into the pan with the shallots and cook, stirring constantly with a wooden spoon, for 2 to 3 minutes until it thickens.

Add the flour all at once, reduce the heat to low, and continue to cook; the dough will start coming together and a thin crust will form at the bottom of the pan. Season with salt, pepper, the cayenne, and nutmeg. Continue cooking, mashing the dough with a wooden spoon until it forms a smooth, glossy paste, 8 to 10 minutes. Transfer to a bowl and cool to room temperature.

Add the Parmesan cheese and mix with a wooden spoon. Using a tablespoon, scoop little mounds of dough, stuff each with a cube of Provolone cheese, and close the balls, pinching with your fingers and rolling in your hands to make 1-inch balls.

Pour the vegetable oil into a heavy bottomed pot or casserole and heat to 350°F, as measured by a deep-fat thermometer. If you don't have a thermometer, pour a drip of batter into the oil; when you hear a sizzling sound and see the batter turning golden brown, the oil is ready. Preheat the oven to 200°F.

While the oil is heating, place the egg in a shallow bowl and the breadcrumbs in another. Pass each *bolinha* into the eggs, then the breadcrumbs, shaking off the excess.

Add the *bolinhas* to the oil in batches, only adding as many as will fit without touching each other. Fry, turning them occasionally so they brown evenly on all sides, about 3 minutes. Transfer to a baking sheet covered with paper towels. Keep the finished batches in a warm oven on a baking sheet until all are fried.

Camarão Assado aos Sabores do Brazil
ROASTED GARLIC-GINGER SHRIMP WITH COCONUT AND FRESH HERB CRUMBS

On a recent trip to Paraty, I came across a fishing boat with shrimp for sale. I bought a few pounds and asked the fisherman for an idea on how to cook my crustaceans. He said, *"Oh Senhora, eu uso os nossos temperos, ponho no forno, e fica uma delícia"* (Oh lady, I use Brazilian seasonings and it comes out delicious). As first I was unhappy with his vague answer, but then the words *nosso temperos* kept circling in my mind. After all, we have tons of spices. I usually stick to shrimp recipes that pair them with another main ingredient, such as pasta with shrimp, rice with shrimp, and shrimp moqueca, but this time I wanted to cook the shrimp by themselves, and this dish, bright and boldly flavored with the Brazilian seasonings, is now my favorite solo shrimp recipe.

SERVES 4

4 tablespoons dendê oil, plus more for greasing (you can substitute olive oil)

6 gloves garlic, minced

1 tablespoon grated fresh ginger

1 scallion, white and green parts, finely chopped

1 tablespoon chopped fresh parsley

1 tablespoon chopped fresh cilantro

½ teaspoon minced jalapeño pepper

Kosher salt

2 pounds large shrimp, peeled and deveined, tails left on

HERB CRUMB

4 tablespoons dendê oil

½ cup toasted manioc flour (*farinha de mandioca*) or breadcrumbs

⅓ cup unsweetened grated coconut

2 tablespoons chopped fresh parsley

2 tablespoons chopped fresh cilantro

½ cup dry white wine

Preheat the oven to 375°F.

In a large bowl, combine the dendê oil with the garlic, ginger, scallion, parsley, cilantro, jalapeño, and salt to taste.

Add the shrimp and toss everything together. Cover and refrigerate for 10 minutes.

Make the herb crumb: In a small bowl, combine the dendê oil with the manioc flour, coconut, parsley, cilantro, and salt to taste.

Lightly grease a 9 x 13-inch baking dish. Lay each shrimp in the dish with the backside flat like a book and the tail end standing straight up. Pour in the wine, then sprinkle the crumb mixture loosely over the shrimp. Place the dish in the oven and roast until the shrimp turn bright orange, 12 to 15 minutes. Serve immediately.

Bolo de Caipirinha com Côco
CAIPIRINHA COCONUT CAKE

On a visit to Paraty where I sampled a variety of different cachaças, I started to think of the desserts I could make using the flavors of caipirinha. Dancing in my head were visions of tender caipirinha cake, exploding with Brazilian flavors. Lime, cachaça, butter, eggs, and coconut milk were no brainers. I turned to Rose Levy Beranbaum for a little tech support, and was rewarded with a nutty, light, gently flavored caipirinha cake. When it was all gone I immediately wanted to make it again and invited some friends over for dinner as an excuse. This time coconut milk was sold out at the supermarket and only cream of coconut was available. I made the cake with the cream of coconut, sneaking a spoonful for quality control purposes. The flavor was markedly different from the previous batch, more creamy, perhaps because of the extra fat from the cream of coconut.

Then I decided my cake needed to get drunk, so I made a caipirinha syrup, and to round out my creation I came up with a caipirinha whipped cream. The cake was so much fun to make and so easy to eat we nearly devoured it all in one sitting. I nicknamed it Caipi-Coco Cake, and it is now a typical Saturday night dessert in my house—along with caipirinhas, of course.

SERVES 8-10

⅔ cup cream of coconut

3 large egg whites

2 tablespoons cachaça

1 teaspoon lemon extract

⅓ cup plus 1 tablespoon sugar

½ cup unsweetened grated coconut

Finely grated zest of 1 lime

1½ cup plus 1 tablespoon cake flour (I use Swans Down)

2¼ teaspoons baking powder

½ teaspoon salt

10 tablespoons unsalted butter

½ cup unsweetened coconut flakes for topping

Preheat the oven to 350°F. Butter a 9 x 2-inch round cake pan, line the bottom with parchment paper, coat the parchment with butter, and dust with flour, tapping out the excess.

In a medium bowl, combine the cream of coconut, egg whites, cachaça, and lemon extract and whisk until well combined.

In a food processor, combine the sugar, grated coconut, and lime zest and process until the oils from the coconut and lime zest infuse the sugar, about 1 minute.

Sift the flour, baking powder, and salt into a large bowl.

In the bowl of an electric mixer fitted with the paddle attachment, cream the butter with the coconut-lime-sugar mixture at medium speed until light and creamy, about 3 minutes, stopping and scraping the sides of the bowl occasionally.

Reduce the speed to low and add half of the cream of coconut mixture—the batter will curdle, and that's okay, as it will come together when you add the remaining ingredients. Continue beating slowly.

Add half of the dry ingredients, alternating with the remaining coconut mixture (begin with the liquid and end with the dry ingredients) and beat until just combined, scraping the sides of the bowl. Scrape the batter into the prepared pan and smooth with an offset spatula.

Bake until golden brown and the sides start to pull from the pan and a tester inserted in the center comes out clean, 30 to 40 minutes.

CAIPIRINHA SYRUP

½ cup sugar

¼ cup lime juice

2 tablespoons cachaça

CAIPI-COCO WHIPPED CREAM

1½ cups heavy cream

1 to 2 tablespoons confectioners' sugar, sifted

1 teaspoon cachaça

Finely grated zest of 1 lime

Meanwhile, make the caipirinha syrup: Combine the sugar and lime juice in a small saucepan and gently warm over low heat, whisking constantly until the sugar is dissolved, about 4 minutes. Don't let it boil. Transfer to a bowl and add the cachaça.

Transfer the cake pan to a wire rack and reduce the oven heat to 300°F. Immediately poke the cake several times with a thin skewer and brush the cake with the syrup (it's important to soak the cake while still hot). Cool inside the pan for at least 30 minutes, then invert onto a serving plate.

While the cake is cooling, spread the coconut flakes on a small baking sheet and toast in the oven until lightly browned, 4 to 6 minutes.

Make the caipi-coco whipped cream: In the bowl of an electric mixer fitted with the whisk attachment, beat the cream with the confectioners' sugar until soft peaks form. Turn off the mixer, add the cachaça and lime zest, and whisk them in by hand. Spread the cream on top of the cake and sprinkle evenly with the toasted coconut. Serve immediately.

11

REGIAO SERRANA

A TRIBUTE TO TERESÓPOLIS IN REGIANO SERRANA

A few miles and a world away north of Rio lies a city called Teresópolis. Part of the mountain region that serves as the weekend getaway for many cariocas, Teresópolis is slightly shadowed by its sister cities Petrópolis and Itaipava. The trio has much in common in terms of offering a weekend of fun and retreat to cariocas, and many people transit from one city to another during the weekend.

Petrópolis, for instance, has a lovely museum, interesting local boutiques, and nice restaurants. Teresópolis, although with fewer spotlights, was a larger part of my childhood. It's a city where nature still calls the shots. There isn't much to do or see, but there is a lot to eat.

Right from the city's entrance, you can hear the sound of running water. It's Fonte Judite, a fountain with water so clean that people bring gallon jugs to fill them up and take with them. Over the mountains we see the tallest peak, called Dedo de Deus ("Finger of God"), the portal of the city. Gargantuan pointy evergreens are everywhere, giving the tree line a jagged edge, like a serrated knife.

The fact that this city offers a colder climate brings a whole different gastronomic culture over the mountains. While in Rio salads, juices, and light meals have an all-year-long appeal,

in Teresópolis the cold climate gives one an opportunity to binge on comfort foods, chocolate desserts, and hot drinks like the Brazilian mallomars (page 176) from Maria Torta and the Brazilian "tiramisu" (page 172) that I include here. The *feirinha*, or outdoor market, provides a natural theater for these feasts, where local foodies and artisans showcase their talents.

The city has a unique spirit, one that beckons to a progressive and outdoorsy group. People share a fondness for bikes, beards, tattoos, flannels, and all-weather pullovers that lie far outside the norm of Rio.

Perhaps it's because I grew up coming here, perhaps it's because the city hasn't changed much since then, but I still feel the wind rippling and wet air from my childhood in Teresópolis.

Caldo de Piranha
PIRANHA SOUP

RESTAURANT: Caldo da Piranha, Rua Jose Elias Zaquem, 350 – Teresopolis

It's hard to imagine a restaurant in Teresópolis serving food from the midwest of Brazil. But in Caldo da Piranha, Mr. Ernani Antonio de Oliveira's traditional restaurant established in 1994, this soup is a specialty. Though Mr. Oliveira does not claim the creation of this recipe, his restaurant's popularity was built upon it. Twenty-five years ago he caught and cooked the dangerous piranha fish for the first time on a trip to Pantanal. He followed a well-known recipe, but as time went by, he perfected his own version, found a supplier in Vitória, Espírito Santo, and sold the dish in his son's snack bar. The success was instant, and his son, transformed his bar into a restaurant specializing in his father's signature dish.

When I tasted the famous soup, I quickly understood how deeply pleasing are the prized flavors of the piranha; with a rich creaminess that comes without the addition of cream, this hearty and earthy soup can be served as an appetizer or as a main course.

SERVES 4

1 whole Branzino, gutted, scaled, head and tail off (about 1½ pounds)

Kosher salt and freshly ground black pepper

4 tablespoons olive oil

3 garlic cloves, chopped

1 small onion, chopped

3 scallions, white and green parts, finely chopped

3 plum tomatoes, peeled, seeded, and chopped

3 tablespoons all-purpose flour

1 tablespoon chopped fresh parsley

1 tablespoon chopped fresh cilantro

Cut the fish into large chunks and season with salt and pepper.

In a large Dutch oven, heat 2 tablespoons of the olive oil over medium heat. Add the fish and cook, turning occasionally, until it starts to turn opaque, about 4 minutes. Depending on the fish, the skin might stick to the bottom of the pan, and that's okay; you can scrape it later. Add enough water to cover the fish, about 3 cups, cover the pan, and bring to boil. Reduce the heat to low and simmer gently until the fish is cooked through, about 5 minutes, skimming off any foam that bubbles to the surface.

Using a slotted spoon, transfer the fish to a bowl. When cool enough to handle, finely shred the fish, discarding the skin and bones, and cover with foil. Strain the liquid and reserve it in a separate bowl.

In the same pan, heat the remaining 2 tablespoons olive oil over low heat, add the garlic, and cook until lightly browned, about 2 minutes. Add the onion and scallions and cook, stirring frequently, until they are softened, about 3 minutes. Add the tomatoes and cook until they just start to release their liquid, 2 to 3 minutes. Season lightly with salt and pepper. Transfer to a food processor (a mini food processor if you have one) and process until smooth, about 1 minute. Scrape back into the same pan.

Add the flour and cook for 1 to 2 minutes over medium heat. Pour in the reserved liquid from the fish, whisking well, and simmer the soup until it thickens, about 10 minutes, adding a little more water if it gets too thick. Add the shredded fish and season with salt and pepper.

To serve, ladle the soup into individual soup bowls and garnish with the parsley and cilantro. (The soup can be kept covered in the refrigerator for up to 2 days. It reheats very well.)

INGREDIENT NOTE: You can make this soup using fish fillet instead of whole fish. In this case, add 3 cups of fish, shrimp, or chicken stock, since you won't be making your own fish stock. Since chances are slim that we'll find piranha outside Brazil, I used branzino here; red snapper and pompano can also work.

Porco na Cerveja
PORK IN BEER

RESTAURANT: Vila St. Gallen
Rua Augusto do Amaral Peixoto,
166 – Teresopolis

Teresópolis, a mountain city one hour north of Rio, has a new attraction: Vila St. Gallen, an artisanal brewery and restaurant specializing in German beer and food. In Rio beer has always been associated with a toast—a reward of a finished project, the gorgeous beaches of Rio, or simply the celebration of life. There is plenty to celebrate with a beer in a glass. But after a visit to Vila St. Gallen, I began to appreciate the potential of using beer as an ingredient.

Beer works nicely with meat, so, inspired by Villa, I came up with this pork in beer stew. I developed this recipe using the beer from Villa St. Galen, but you can use any full-bodied beer in this recipe. I wanted to get my pork completely drunk, so I marinated it overnight to infuse the meat with that sweet and bitter beer taste. Then I lightly browned the pork and braised it in the oven with aromatic vegetables and new potatoes as an accompaniment.

SERVES 4–6

2 pounds boneless pork shoulder or butt, excess fat removed, cut into 1-inch chunks

1 large onion, quartered

2 celery stalks, cut into large chunks

2 medium carrots, cut into large chunks

3 garlic cloves, lightly crushed

3 fresh bay leaves

Two 11.2-ounce bottles of beer, like Stella Artois

Kosher salt and freshly ground black pepper

3 tablespoons extra virgin olive oil, plus more if needed

5 plum tomatoes, peeled, seeded, and roughly chopped

4 cups chicken stock

1½ pounds small new potatoes, peeled and quartered

3 tablespoons chopped fresh parsley

Place the pork, onion, celery, carrots, garlic, and bay leaves in a large zip-top bag. Pour in the beer, distribute well in the bag, and seal it, making sure all the air is out. Marinate in the refrigerator for at least 4 hours, or preferably overnight.

Preheat the oven to 350°F.

Separate the pork from the vegetables and strain the liquid. Reserve all. Place the pork on a baking sheet lined with paper towels and air dry for 5 minutes. Pat dry to remove any excess moisture. Season with salt and pepper.

Pour the beer into a small saucepan and bring to a boil over medium heat. Foam will rise to the surface; skim and remove it and cook until ½ cup to ¾ cup is left, 4 to 5 minutes. Strain over a measuring cup.

Heat the olive oil in a large, deep skillet or Dutch oven over high heat and, working in batches if necessary, sear the pork until lightly browned all over, about 4 minutes. Transfer to a bowl and cover with aluminum foil to keep moist.

Reduce the heat to low and add the vegetables to the pan, adding more oil if necessary. Season lightly with salt and pepper and cook, stirring with a wooden spoon and scraping the browned bits from the bottom of the pan, until the vegetables are softened and translucent, about 5 minutes.

Add the tomatoes and cook until softened, about 2 minutes. Season lightly with salt and pepper. Add the beer and chicken stock and bring to a boil over high heat.

Add the pork and any juices accumulated in the bowl. Cover the pan, place in the oven, and braise for 1 hour. Discard the large pieces of carrots and celery (I leave the onions), add the potatoes, cover, and continue to braise until the pork is very tender and the potatoes are just tender, 30 to 35 minutes. Garnish with the parsley and serve.

Panquecas de Espinafre
SPINACH CRÊPES WITH FRESH TOMATO SAUCE

Ivani de Souza Ferreira is a woman who makes a living from the art of cooking. She grew up around food and learned to cook by watching other people, so when I asked if she could share a recipe for this book, I was expecting she would have at least a notebook with recipes archived. But everything she cooks comes straight from the bank of knowledge she has inside her head; she never follows a recipe. The best part about cooking with her is tapping into that knowledge there in the kitchen. More about that in the next recipe. This one that Ivani shared is healthy, light, nutritious, and super delicious! Take this recipe as a guideline; from here you can add different mushrooms or Gorgonzola or your choice of additional ingredients to the spinach.

SERVES 4–6 OR
MAKES 8–10 CRÊPES

½ cup all-purpose flour

½ cup whole milk

¼ cup lukewarm water

2 tablespoons unsalted butter, melted and cooled

2 large eggs, lightly beaten

½ teaspoon kosher salt

Olive oil, for cooking the crêpes

SPINACH FILLING

2 tablespoons salt, plus more for seasoning

10 ounces fresh spinach

1 tablespoon unsalted butter

2 garlic cloves, minced

1 small shallot, minced

¾ cup chicken stock

2 tablespoons all-purpose flour

Freshly ground black pepper

Freshly grated nutmeg

In a blender, combine the flour, milk, water, butter, eggs, and salt and blend until the batter is very smooth, 1 to 2 minutes. Transfer to a bowl, cover, and refrigerate for at least 30 minutes.

Meanwhile, make the spinach filling: In a large saucepan, bring 1 quart of water to a boil and add the salt. Trim any thick stems from the spinach. Add the spinach to the boiling water and cook until just softened, about 1 minute. Drain the spinach into a colander and press on it to remove excess liquid. Let the spinach continue to drain for 5 minutes, then roughly chop it.

In a medium saucepan, melt the butter. Add the garlic and cook until just golden, about 1 minute. Add the shallot and cook until softened, another minute. Stir in the spinach, then remove the pan from the heat.

In a small saucepan, heat the chicken stock over low heat. Place the flour in a small bowl, add a few tablespoons of the stock, and whisk well. Pour the mixture back into the chicken stock and cook, whisking constantly, until it starts to thicken, about 3 minutes. Season with salt, pepper, and nutmeg. Mix the spinach into the chicken stock. Taste again, adjust the seasonings if necessary, and remove from the heat.

Make the tomato sauce: In a medium saucepan, melt the butter over low heat and add the garlic; cook until just golden, about 1 minute. Add the onion and cook until softened, about 5 minutes. Add the tomatoes and cook, stirring frequently, until they begin to soften, another 2 minutes. Add the water, increase the heat to medium, bring to a boil, and then add the tomato sauce. Season with salt and pepper. Cook until nice and tasty, 10 to 15 minutes.

Preheat the oven to 350°F. Grease a 9 x 13-inch baking dish with butter.

Heat a small nonstick skillet over low heat. Add about 1 teaspoon olive oil and swirl the pan around to coat the bottom. Pour in 2 to 3 tablespoons of the batter and immediately swirl the pan to spread the batter into a thin even circle. Cook until the bottom side turns gorgeously golden brown, about 2 minutes (take a peek), then using an offset spatula, flip and cook the other side until you see black spots,

TOMATO SAUCE

1 tablespoon butter

2 garlic cloves, minced

½ onion, chopped

2 plum tomatoes, peeled, seeded, and diced

½ cup water

One 15-ounce can tomato sauce

Kosher salt and freshly ground black pepper

½ cup freshly grated Parmesan cheese

another 2 minutes (the second side is never as pretty as the first). Transfer to a baking sheet and repeat with the remaining batter.

Fill each crêpe with 2 to 3 tablespoons of spinach, then roll it tightly. Arrange the crêpes on the prepared baking dish and spoon some tomato sauce on top. (You might not use all of the tomato sauce.) Sprinkle the Parmesan on top and bake until the cheese is melted and the sauce is bubbling, about 12 minutes. Serve immediately.

COOKING TIP: If you want to add a bit more flavor to the topping, try substituting Gruyère for the Parmesan cheese. You can also use frozen spinach; if you do so, simply thaw it rather than blanch it. You can prepare the dish ahead of time and keep it covered in the refrigerator for up to 2 days.

Empadão de Palmito da Ivani
IVANI'S HEARTS OF PALM TART

In cooking school I learned how to make chicken stock and veal stock and all the other foundational stocks. In the professional world bouillon cubes are looked at with disdain. When I watched Ivani de Souza Ferreira prepare this wonderful tart, my world turned upside down when I saw her using a bouillon cube in it. At first I just couldn't grasp what she was doing. I kept asking her, "Where is the water? Aren't you going to dissolve it in water?" She just looked at me, smiled, and continued cooking. From that day on, the bouillon cube has become one of my favorite seasonings.

SERVES 6-8

DOUGH

3⅓ cups all-purpose flour, plus more for rolling

1 teaspoon salt

1 cup (2 sticks) plus 2 tablespoons unsalted butter

3 large egg yolks

4 tablespoons water

HEARTS OF PALM FILLING

1 cup whole milk

3 tablespoons all-purpose flour

Kosher salt and freshly ground black pepper

2 tablespoons unsalted butter

4 garlic cloves, minced

1 onion, chopped

3 plum tomatoes peeled, seeded, and diced

1 cube chicken bouillon (preferably Knorr)

1½ pounds hearts of palm, sliced into ¼-inch-thick rings (about four 14-ounce cans)

2 tablespoons chopped green olives (optional)

Make the dough: Combine the flour and salt in the bowl of a food processor. Add the butter and pulse until it looks like coarse meal. Add the egg yolks and water and continue to pulse until the dough just starts to come together (depending on humidity, you might need a few drops more of water). Place the dough on a floured surface and gather it into a ball; divide it in half and shape it into 2 flat disks. Wrap in plastic wrap and refrigerate for at least 30 minutes (this can be done up to 2 days ahead).

Next, make the filling: In a small saucepan, warm the milk over low heat. Place the flour in a small bowl, add 2 to 3 tablespoons of the milk, and whisk well to dissolve. Pour back into the saucepan and cook over low heat, whisking constantly, until thickened, about 3 minutes. Season with salt and pepper. Remove from the heat, cover, and set aside.

In a medium saucepan, melt the butter over low heat, add the garlic, and cook until just starting to turn golden, about 2 minutes. Add the onion and cook until softened, about 2 minutes. Add the tomatoes and cook until everything blends, about 3 minutes. Crumble in the bouillon cube and mix well with a wooden spatula to dissolve it. Add the hearts of palm and fold everything together. Add the green olives, if using, and the parsley and season lightly with salt and pepper.

Pour the thickened milk into the hearts of palm mixture and fold it in. Taste again and adjust the seasoning if needed. Spread the mixture into a baking sheet and refrigerate for at least 30 minutes (this can be prepared up to 2 days ahead of time).

Remove the dough from the refrigerator at least 20 minutes before rolling it so that it becomes malleable. On a lightly floured surface, roll the first piece of dough into a circle 1/16 inch thick, lifting the dough often and making sure that the work surface and the dough are amply floured at all times. Roll the dough up and around your rolling pin, then unroll it into a 9-inch springform pan, fitting the dough into the bottom and up the sides of the pan. If the dough cracks or splits as you work, don't worry—you can patch the cracks with scraps using a wet finger to "glue" them in place.

Spoon the filling evenly across the dough. Using a pastry brush dipped in water, lightly moisten the exposed edges of the bottom

½ cup chopped fresh parsley

1 large egg, beaten, for the egg wash

crust. Roll the top crust into a circle and transfer to the top of the mold, pressing against the bottom crust with your fingers, then trim the overhang from both crusts, making sure the two crusts are securely sealed together.

Cut an X in the center to serve as a steam vent. Refrigerate for at least 20 minutes before baking.

Position a rack at the center of the oven and preheat the oven to 375°F. Place the tart on a baking sheet and bake until the top is lightly browned, about 30 minutes. Remove the tart from the oven, brush the top with egg wash, return to the oven, and bake until the crust is gorgeously browned, 10 to 15 minutes more. Transfer to a rack, let rest for 20 minutes before serving, and serve warm.

Strudel de Frango com Catupiry
SAVORY STRUDELS WITH CHICKEN AND CATUPIRY CHEESE

When he arrived in Petrópolis, German immigrant Stefano Kern brought to Rio recipes from his native land. Together with other bakers, he opened Casa do Alemão. The first store opened on the highway from Rio to the mountain region, cariocas on their way out of the city regularly make this sacred stop at Casa do Alemão to eat their favorite snacks. This recipe is inspired by this German-carioca establishment. If you're wondering why you have to make two strudels instead of one, it's because the proportion of dough to filling just doesn't work with one large strudel. But this is not an easy recipe easy to cut in half, so I decided to make the strudel thinner and more elegant by splitting the dough—it's easier to handle, easier to bake, and easier to present. You have the option of serving one strudel right away and keeping the other on a baking sheet covered in plastic in the refrigerator for up to 2 days before baking.

MAKES 2; SERVES 6–8

2½ cups (about 1 pound) shredded cooked chicken

2 tablespoons olive oil

1 onion, finely chopped

1 celery stalk, finely chopped

3 garlic cloves, minced

2 plum tomatoes, peeled, seeded, and diced, or 5 tablespoons prepared marinara sauce

2 teaspoons dried oregano

Kosher salt and freshly ground black pepper

Freshly grated nutmeg

2 tablespoons chopped fresh parsley

¾ cup chicken stock

1 tablespoon butter

2 tablespoons all-purpose flour, plus more for dusting

Place the shredded chicken in a large bowl.

In a medium skillet, heat the olive oil over medium-low heat, add the onion and celery, and cook until softened and translucent, about 3 minutes. Add the garlic and cook for another minute. Add the tomatoes and oregano and cook until the tomatoes are softened. Season with salt, pepper, and nutmeg. Pour on top of the chicken, add the parsley, and mix well.

Warm the chicken stock in a small saucepan. In another pan, melt the butter over low heat. Immediately add the flour and cook until it starts to bubble lightly. Add the chicken stock and whisk vigorously, making sure there are no lumps. Season lightly with salt, pepper, and nutmeg. Add to the chicken mixture and combine well. Taste and adjust the seasoning one more time. Refrigerate until cold. (You can make this filling up to 2 days ahead; keep covered in the refrigerator.)

Open the puff pastry onto a floured surface. Using a rolling pin, roll the dough into a 12 x 18-inch rectangle. Slide the dough onto a baking sheet and refrigerate for 10 minutes.

Remove the dough from the refrigerator and cut vertically into 2 strips of 6 x 18 inches. Arrange each piece of dough onto a sheet of parchment paper dusted lightly with flour for easy transfer to the baking sheet. Distribute the chicken filling equally and vertically along the two pieces of dough, leaving a 2-inch border on all sides. Using a spoon, create a vertical path to receive the Catupiry cheese. Place the Catupiry cheese inside a pastry bag without a tip (or a zip-top bag with the corner cut off) and squeeze a thick line of cheese right in the middle of the filling. Using a spatula, push some of the chicken on top to cover the cheese, keeping it from touching the dough.

RESTAURANT: Casa do Alemão
Estr. Ayrton Senna, 927 –
Petrópolis casadoalemao.com.br

14 ounces ready-made puff pastry (I use Du Four)

8 ounces Catupiry cheese, at room temperature

1 large egg, beaten, for the egg wash

Brush the edges of the dough with egg wash. Bring one side of the dough closest to you over the filling and then bring the opposite dough over the filling to meet and overlap the first piece of dough. Fold both ends of each strudel, pressing the dough to the bottom and encasing the filling. Brush off any excess flour. Quickly flip the strudel onto the baking sheet seam side down. Repeat with the second piece of dough. Chill for at least 1 hour before baking.

Preheat the oven to 375°F.

Brush the strudels with egg wash and bake until the dough is crisp and golden brown, 30 to 35 minutes, rotating once during baking time. Some of the filling will ooze out as the strudels bake, and that's okay.

Remove the strudels from the oven and cool on the baking sheet for at least 20 minutes before serving. Cut into slices and serve warm.

Pavê de Bombom
BRAZILIAN "TIRAMISU"

This recipe comes from Juliana Ferreira Gaspar, a young woman who loves to bake. I met her through her mother Ivani, who loves to cook savory dishes and calls on her daughter when it comes to baking. Mother and daughter make a great team. This recipe, a classic in Rio, is a cross between trifle and tiramisu and you can assemble it either in a baking dish or a trifle. Juliana makes this recipe using Maria's cookies (a brand of sweet crackers), but I prefer the absorbing power of ladyfingers. The chocolate sauce is my added touch to the recipe; feel free to omit it to keep to the original recipe.

SERVES 8–10

CHOCOLATE SAUCE

1 cup whole milk

½ cup heavy cream

2 tablespoons unsalted butter

¼ cup plus 2 tablespoons sugar

10½ ounces semisweet chocolate, chopped

PASTRY CREAM

4 cups whole milk

One 14-ounce can sweetened condensed milk

5 large egg yolks

2 tablespoons all-purpose flour

2 tablespoons cornstarch

1 cup heavy cream

14 Serenata do Amor bonbons or 16 Reese's Peanut Butter Cups (see Note)

2 tablespoons unsweetened cocoa powder, plus more for garnish

1 tablespoon Cointreau liquor (optional)

36 ladyfingers (preferably Italian Savoiardi)

First make the chocolate sauce: In a medium saucepan, combine the milk, heavy cream, butter, and sugar, place over medium heat, and bring to a boil. Add the chocolate and cook, whisking constantly, until the chocolate melts and the mixture comes to a boil. Continue to whisk vigorously for about 5 minutes, until creamy, making sure to whisk around the sides and corners of the pan to avoid uneven cooking. Transfer to a bowl and cool to room temperature, stirring occasionally. You will only need ½ cup of this sauce; freeze the rest in a plastic storage container to use over ice cream. (This can be done up to 1 week ahead; reheat until melted.)

Next, make the pastry cream: In a medium saucepan, combine 2 cups of the whole milk and the condensed milk and cook over medium heat until hot.

In a medium bowl, whisk the egg yolks. Sift the flour and cornstarch over the yolks and whisk until blended and thickened. Gently pour about half of the hot milk mixture into the yolks to prevent curdling, whisk well, then add the remaining milk. Strain the mixture back to the saucepan and cook over very low heat, whisking constantly (make sure to get into the edges of the pan), until it takes on a custard consistency, 5 to 8 minutes. Cool to room temperature, stirring occasionally.

In the bowl of an electric mixer fitted with the whisk attachment, whip the heavy cream on medium to high speed until soft peaks forms. Fold the whipped cream into the pastry cream and refrigerate until you're ready to assemble the dessert.

Place the bonbons in the bowl of a food processor and pulse until it looks like coarse meal. Set aside.

In a small saucepan, bring the remaining 2 cups milk to a boil over medium heat. Reduce the heat and whisk in the cocoa powder until it is completely dissolved. Pour into a bowl and cool to room temperature. If you're adding the Cointreau, add it now.

Dip each ladyfinger into the milk, hold it there for 2 seconds, then lay them in a trifle bowl. Drizzle a little of chocolate sauce over them in a zigzag pattern. Pour in half of the pastry cream and spread with a spatula. Sprinkle over half of the crumbled bonbons. Repeat with the remaining ladyfingers, chocolate sauce, pastry cream, and bonbons.

VANILLA ICING

2 large egg whites

Small pinch of salt

2 tablespoons sugar

1 cup heavy cream

1 teaspoon vanilla extract

Refrigerate while you prepare the icing. Alternatively, assemble the dish in a 9 x 13-inch baking dish; your two layers will be longer.

Prepare the icing: In an electric mixer fitted with the whisk attachment, beat the egg whites with the salt. When the whites start to foam, gradually sprinkle in the sugar and beat until soft peaks form. In another bowl, also with the whisk attachment, whip the heavy cream to soft peaks. When you're almost there, add the vanilla and give it a quick whisk by hand. Fold the two together and pour on top of the tiramisu, swirling with an offset spatula. Refrigerate for at least 4 hours or preferably overnight before serving and bring to room temperature 20 minutes before serving.

INGREDIENT NOTE: In Rio we use Brazilian chocolate candies called Serenata do Amor or Sonho de Valsa (Juliana crumbles them by hand), but in the United States, when I can't find them I like to use Reese's Peanut Butter Cups because it has the closest flavors to the Brazilian candies, and I chop it by hand. You will need around 16.

Mousse de Morango
TRIPLE STRAWBERRY MOUSSE

Fruit in Brazil is hugely abundant, so Brazilians are always incorporating fruit into desserts. Here you have a triple dose of strawberries presented in a light but sumptuous mousse. While I prefer to make the mousse with fresh strawberries, you can use frozen pulp or frozen strawberries; just make sure to thaw them completely and bring them to room temperature before blending. Have a lemon or lime nearby—if needed, you can brighten up the flavor of the fruit with just a few drops of acidity.

SERVES 8–10

MOUSSE

Canola oil for greasing

1½ pounds strawberries, rinsed and hulled

½ cup sugar

½ cup water

2 envelopes powdered gelatin

1⅔ cups heavy cream

STRAWBERRY SAUCE

8 ounces strawberries, rinsed and hulled

½ cup sugar

Few drops of lemon juice if needed

More strawberries for garnish

SPECIAL EQUIPMENT:
One 8-cup tube pan

Prepare the mousse: Grease an 8-cup tube pan with canola oil.

Combine the strawberries and sugar in a blender and blend until pureed. Strain over a measuring cup, pressing on the solids—you should have about 2¼ cups of strawberry puree. Transfer to a large bowl.

Pour the water into a small saucepan, sprinkle the gelatin over it, and whisk to dissolve. Let sit for 5 minutes. Add about ½ cup of the strawberry puree and cook over low heat without letting it boil, whisking constantly until the gelatin dissolves. Pour into the strawberry puree and whisk well.

Place the heavy cream in the bowl of an electric mixer fitted with the whisk attachment. Beat on medium-high speed until you see traces of the whisk holding the cream. Carefully fold the whipped cream into the strawberry puree until well combined. Carefully transfer the mousse to the prepared tube pan, using a spatula to spread it evenly. Cover and refrigerate for at least 6 hours or preferably overnight.

Make the strawberry sauce: Combine the strawberries and sugar in a blender and blend until pureed. Strain over a measuring cup, pressing on the solids—you should have about 1½ cups of strawberry puree. Taste and add a few drops of lemon juice if necessary to brighten the flavor.

Remove the mousse from the refrigerator and run a knife along the edges of the tube pan. Invert the pan onto a platter and tap the pan so the mousse slides out. Carefully lift the pan. Pour the strawberry sauce over and around the mousse and garnish with whole strawberries.

Pudim de Pão com Doce de Leite
DULCE DE LECHE BRIOCHE PUDDING

I love chocolate bread pudding, and when I came across the many varieties of homemade dulce de leite found all over the mountain region around Rio, I decided to play with this ingredient in my bread pudding. This recipe gives you a satiny, sweet, bright caramel puddle that will put a smile on your face. I like to serve mine with coconut ice cream, but vanilla would do just as well. It is important to use brioche (challah can also work), as it keeps its form while absorbing the liquid from the custard.

SERVES 4–6

⅓ cup plus 1 tablespoon whole milk

1⅔ cups heavy cream

6 tablespoons sugar

6 large egg yolks

Salt

1 cup prepared dulce de leche (I use Nestle)

3 tablespoons dark rum

¼ teaspoon ground cinnamon

⅛ teaspoon freshly grated nutmeg

4 slices brioche, crusts cut off, cut into ¼-inch cubes (about 3 cups)

Store-bought coconut ice cream (optional)

Lightly coat a 7 x 11-inch baking dish with cooking spray.

In a medium saucepan, combine the milk, cream, and 3 tablespoons of the sugar and bring to a boil over medium heat.

In a medium bowl, whisk the egg yolks with the remaining 3 tablespoons sugar and a small pinch of salt. Slowly pour in a little of the hot milk mixture to temper the yolks, then pour in the rest, whisking all the while.

Place the dulce de leche in a small glass bowl and warm it up slightly in the microwave for 40 seconds or so. Add it to the yolk mixture and whisk well until the dulce de leche is completely "melted" and the mixture is homogeneous.

Add the rum, cinnamon, and nutmeg and whisk well.

Spread the brioche over the bottom of the prepared baking dish. Pour the liquid mixture over it, making sure every piece of bread is well covered (push it down; as it absorbs liquid it will sink). Leave the pan at room temperature for 30 minutes to allow the bread to absorb the liquid before baking.

Meanwhile, preheat the oven to 350°F.

Bake the pudding until it is slightly jiggly, about 20 minutes (12 to 14 minutes for individual puddings). Transfer to a wire rack and let rest for 10 minutes. Serve warm with a scoop of coconut ice cream if you like.

COOKING TIP: For a fancier presentation, you can prepare this recipe using 8 individual 4-ounce foil cups.

Nhá Benta
BRAZILIAN MALLOMARS

RESTAURANT: Maria Torta Café
R. Manuel Madruga, 8 - Teresopolis
mariatorta.com.br

In a tiny store called Maria Torta located in Teresópolis, I discovered a version of *nhá benta* that rose above the kind I grew up with. Bite into the chocolate shell-like crust and there is a surrender to the perfect combination of a slightly sweet creamy marshmallow mountain atop a crumbly cookie. They use a local cookie that is hard to find anywhere else but very easy to replace. Here I like to use small and crunchy vanilla wafer cookies, and for the coating, I use baker's chocolate to give it a nice shiny coating without making the chocolate too hard to crack (see Note below). Maria Torta doesn't use gelatin in their recipe, which results in a fresh and creamy meringue, but this also means it's more perishable. After 3 to 4 days left at room temperature, you might see some water leak out of the cookie, which is fine by me, because they never last that long anyway. At Maria Torta they pipe the meringue with a star pastry tip, but I prefer a more modern look using a round pastry tip.

MAKES ABOUT 42

3 large egg whites

⅔ cup sugar

⅛ teaspoon salt

1 teaspoon vanilla extract

42 vanilla wafer cookies
    (1½ inches in diameter)

2 pounds baker's chocolate,
    chopped

Combine the egg whites, sugar, and salt in the bowl of an electric mixer set over a pot of simmering water (the bowl should not touch the water). Whisk constantly until the mixture is warm to the touch; it should look slightly foamy and the sugar should be completely dissolved.

Bring the bowl to an electric mixer fitted with the whisk attachment and beat on medium-high speed until fluffy, glossy, and completely cooled, about 10 minutes. Add the vanilla and beat until combined.

Line the vanilla cookies on a baking sheet. Scoop the meringue into a pastry bag fitted with a round #4 tip and pipe the meringue on top of each cookie.

Place the chopped chocolate in a bowl set on the top of a pan filled with simmering water (the bowl should not touch the water) and, without leaving the spot, heat the chocolate until it's three-quarters melted, about 5 minutes. Remove the bowl from the simmering water and finish melting it by mixing with a rubber spatula (this prevents the chocolate from getting too hot). Let stand until the glaze cools a little but is still fluid. Drop a meringue cookie into the chocolate glaze and flip to cover the entire outside. Using a chocolate fork, lift it out and let the excess glaze drip off. Place on a baking sheet covered with parchment paper. Repeat until all are covered.

INGREDIENT NOTE: For many years, I looked at baker's chocolate with disdain, believing that a real chocolatier would never use this product, which is chocolate mixed with vegetable fat. But recently baker's chocolate—or pâte à glacer as it's called in the pastry world—has received the attention of some of the finest chocolate brands in the world, and today's version of the product is a lot more refined, flavorful, and easier to find. You don't need to temper baker's chocolate, making it perfect for dipping fresh fruit into. I buy a brand called Felchlin from Swiss Chalet Fine Foods (www.scff.com). Cacao Barry also makes a great version, which you can find at www.chocosphere.com. You can make your own baker's chocolate by mixing melted chocolate with vegetable oil in a ratio of 3 tablespoons oil to 12 ounces of chocolate.

12

HOME COOKING

FROM TANGIER TO RIO

When I speak English, most people recognize a foreign accent. Well, sure, I am from Brazil. When my father speaks Portuguese, the same happens. And when my aunt Sarita speaks Portuguese, they think she is a tourist!

Aunt Sarita is my father's oldest sister. She and my father were born in Tangier, Morocco, and immigrated to Brazil in 1960, when my aunt was twenty-two, the same age I was when I moved to New York.

Recently I started to trace back my family's history. What brought them from Tangier to Rio? And where does my affinity for cooking come from? I know for sure it's not from my parents. Although they love to eat, my mother doesn't cook much beyond making fried eggs— something she does quite well—but only because that is one of her favorite foods to eat.

It all started with Aunt Sarita, or Tia Sarita as we say in Portuguese. She came to Brazil in 1958, while the rest of the family stayed in Tangier. Two years later, as the political situation worsened in Morocco, the rest of the family emigrated. My father was eleven years old when he came to Brazil. He still says the word Leblon—one of the most famous neighborhoods in Rio, and where we live —with a French accent. The minute the words leave his lips, cariocas know he wasn't born in Brazil.

As I embarked on a quest to recover my family's recipes, I spent one of the most memorable afternoons of my life cooking with Tia Sarita and Neusa de Souza, an African Brazilian woman who helps my aunt. On a visit to her apartment in Rio de Janeiro, with the typical bright sun reflecting on their veranda, I asked my aunt to show me how to cook like a real Moroccan.

As I watched my aunt cook, I saw myself in her. The way she bends her body when she stirs the ground meat; the way her face hides a smile when the food turns out well; even the way her nose is as pointy as mine. I had no idea that by cooking with her I'd also find a part of myself.

For Tia Sarita, food remains the primary connection between her Moroccan roots and her new life in Brazil. After fifty years of living in Brazil, I can see in both my aunt and my father how Brazil has changed them—for the better. My father's devotion to fitness is a testament to his successful Brazilian acclimation, as is his love for cold beer accompanied by cod fritters and lots of loud friends. My aunt's relationship with Neusa de Souza, the woman who cooks with her and has absorbed the traditions of our family, is testament as well. All that joie de vivre that cariocas are known for has rubbed off on them, and today they are completely immersed in the culture of their adopted country.

TIA SARITA'S MOROCCAN MEATBALLS

It's the combination of Moroccan spices that makes this recipe so interesting. My Aunt Sarita uses two kinds of paprika here: Hungarian, with a sweet taste and a vibrant red color, and smoked Spanish (where peppers are smoked over an oak fire), with a richer taste and a darker red tone.

SERVES 4–6

1 pound ground beef

1 large egg yolk

1 slice whole wheat bread, crusts removed and torn into small pieces

1 onion, minced

¼ teaspoon ground cinnamon

¼ teaspoon ground cumin

½ teaspoon Hungarian paprika

2 teaspoons Spanish paprika

1 teaspoon ground coriander

1 tablespoon chopped fresh parsley

2 tablespoons olive oil

1½ teaspoons kosher salt

Freshly ground black pepper

SAFFRON SAUCE

3 tablespoons olive oil

4 small onions, chopped

1 bay leaf

1½ teaspoons ground ginger

Pinch of saffron

1½ teaspoons ground cumin

½ teaspoon Hungarian paprika

½ teaspoon Spanish paprika

Pinch of ground turmeric

Kosher salt and freshly ground black pepper

Juice of ½ lime

¼ cup chopped fresh parsley

¼ cup chopped fresh cilantro

Place the beef, egg yolk, bread pieces, onion, spices, parsley, olive oil, salt and a grind or two of pepper in a bowl and combine well with a rubber spatula or knead with your hands. Scoop a tiny portion and fry in a small pan to make sure the seasoning is just right. Refrigerate for at least 30 minutes, or preferably 2 hours.

Have a small bowl of water nearby, wet your hands, and form ½-inch balls. Set aside on a plate until ready to cook.

Make the sauce: Warm the olive oil in a large deep saucepan over medium-low heat. Add the onions and cook until softened and translucent, about 6 minutes. Add the bay leaf, ginger, saffron, cumin, Hungarian and Spanish paprika, turmeric, and salt and pepper to taste and cook, stirring frequently with a wooden spoon, until fragrant, 3 to 5 minutes. Add 1½ cups hot water and bring to a boil.

Add the meatballs, reduce the heat to low, cover, and poach them for 20 minutes, stirring halfway through and adding more water if necessary.

Add the lime juice, parsley, and cilantro and stir carefully. Transfer the meatballs and sauce to a serving plate and serve immediately.

Escondidinho de Salmon Com Espinafre
SPINACH AND SALMON SHEPHERD'S PIE

My interest for cooking began when I was eight years old. By twelve, I had already clipped newspaper and magazines recipes by the hundreds. As I grew older, my interest in cooking turned into an obsession. It took me a long time to realize that knowing how to cook was a special skill and something to proud of. No one else my age shared the joy of cooking, at least not where I was from. There was one particular magazine called *Claudia Cozinha* that was my favorite. This recipe is inspired by an article I tore out more than twenty years ago and I still find it makes a delicious dinner. Some recipes never get old.

SERVES 4–6

1½ pounds salmon, skin on

Kosher salt and freshly ground black pepper

5 tablespoons extra virgin olive oil

2 garlic cloves, chopped

½ pound spinach leaves (about 8 cups lightly packed)

Freshly grated nutmeg

1 shallot, chopped

½ cup crème fraîche or sour cream

1 teaspoon Dijon mustard

2 pounds Yukon gold potatoes, peeled and quartered

½ cup whole milk

2 tablespoons unsalted butter, at room temperature

¼ cup freshly grated Parmesan cheese

Preheat the oven to 350°F. Lightly coat a 7 x 11-inch baking dish with oil or cooking spray. Cover a baking sheet with aluminum foil and spray lightly with cooking spray.

Season both sides of the salmon with salt and pepper, drizzle with 1 tablespoon of the olive oil, and place skin side down on the baking sheet. Roast the salmon in the oven until medium-rare, 6 to 8 minutes. Remove the salmon and let cool a little. Flake the salmon into big chunks, place in a bowl, and cover with aluminum foil. You should have approximately 2 cups salmon.

Heat 2 tablespoons of the remaining olive oil in a large skillet over medium heat. Add the garlic and cook until it just starts to turn golden, about 1 minute. Immediately add the spinach leaves and toss everything with a pair of tongs, turning the leaves and bringing the garlic to the surface. Cook until the spinach is wilted, about 2 minutes. Season with salt, pepper, and nutmeg and add to the bowl with the salmon. Cover with foil again.

Wipe any garlic bits from the pan and add the remaining 2 tablespoons olive oil and the shallot. Cook over low heat until just softened, about 2 minutes. Add the crème fraîche and mustard and cook until the crème fraîche is just melted (don't let it boil). Season with salt and pepper. Add to the bowl with the salmon and spinach. Fold everything together, taste, and adjust the seasoning if necessary. Spread the filling onto the prepared baking dish and cover lightly; set aside.

Have a potato ricer or food mill ready. Place the potatoes in a medium pot and fill with cold water to come 1 inch above the potatoes. Add 1 tablespoon salt, partially cover, and bring to a boil. Reduce the heat to medium and cook until the potatoes are fork-tender.

Meanwhile, heat the milk in a small saucepan. When the potatoes are done, immediately drain them into a colander and pass them through the food mill, at the same time adding the hot milk and the butter. Stir the mashed potato with a wooden spoon or rubber spatula and adjust the seasoning with salt. Spoon the potatoes over the salmon-spinach filling and spread evenly with an offset spatula. Sprinkle with the cheese.

Place the dish onto the prepared baking sheet and bake until the edges start to bubble and the top is lightly browned, about 30 minutes. Remove from the oven and let rest for 5 minutes before serving.

Ervilhas com Ovos

FRESH PEAS WITH SUNNY-SIDE UP EGGS AND SAUSAGE

If you like peas, like most Brazilians do, then this dish is for you. It highlights the vegetable in a healthy and delicious way, with the oozing egg yolks over the peas and sausage adding a satisfying touch of luxury. I have made this recipe with success many times using frozen peas, but when I get my hands on fresh peas, it's even better. In Rio I always prepare this dish with linguiça (traditional Brazilian sausage); in the United States, if I cannot get linguiça at a Brazilian store, I use chorizo.

SERVES 4

¾ pound linguiça sausage or chorizo

2 tablespoons extra virgin olive oil

½ onion, chopped

2 garlic cloves, minced

1 pound (3 cups) peas

1 cup of chicken stock or water

Kosher salt and freshly ground black pepper

2 tablespoons unsalted butter

4 large eggs, at room temperature

2 tablespoons chopped fresh parsley

Split the sausages in half lengthwise and cut into ½-inch pieces. Heat the olive oil in a large skillet over medium heat. Add the sausage and cook, stirring occasionally, until all the pieces are slightly crisp, about 5 minutes. Using a slotted spoon, transfer to a bowl and cover with foil to keep moist.

Using the fat rendered from the sausage, add the onions and reduce the heat to low. Cook until softened and translucent, about 2 minutes. Add the garlic and stir. Add the peas and cook until they are warmed through, about 2 minutes. Add the chicken stock and sausage, season with salt and pepper, cover the pan, and simmer for 5 minutes.

Meanwhile, heat a large nonstick skillet over medium heat. Melt the butter and crack in the eggs. Season with salt and pepper and cook the eggs sunny-side up until the whites are cooked but the yolks are still soft and runny. Add the parsley to the skillet with the peas, slide the eggs over the peas, and cook for another minute over low heat. Spoon a mound of peas, sausage, and egg onto individual plates, scooping some of the sauce from the bottom of the skillet on top. Serve immediately.

Carne Moída Com Ovos e Azeitona
GROUND BEEF WITH HARD-BOILED EGGS AND OLIVES

For most of my life I grew up on a tiny street located at the end corner of Leblon, called Rua Aperana. My building faced the oncoming street, and even though I didn't have a view of the beach, we had a view of the beginning of Canal at Rua Visconde de Pirajá, which leads you to other neighborhoods including Jardim Botânico and Gávea.

My life was built around that corner of Leblon, with my after-school activities consisting of learning English twice a week at Ann Arbor English Studies, located just a few steps from Rua Aperana, then a walk to the Columbia gym center. Back home I would always look forward to eating *carne moída com ovos e azeitona* (accompanied by rice and beans, as a good carioca) in the veranda of my apartment. More often than not, this recipe is all that I need to bring those childhood memories back.

SERVES 4

2 large eggs

2 tablespoons extra virgin olive oil

3 garlic cloves, minced

1 small onion, chopped

3 plum tomatoes, peeled, seeded, and diced

2 teaspoons dried oregano

Kosher salt and freshly ground black pepper

½ cube chicken bouillon (I use Knorr)

1 pound ground beef

Freshly grated nutmeg

⅓ cup (about 4 ounces) kalamata olives, pitted and roughly chopped

4 tablespoons chopped fresh parsley

Place the eggs in a small saucepan, cover with cold water, and bring to a boil. Reduce the heat to low and cook until the eggs are hard-cooked. Remove the eggs from the water and shock them in ice water. Peel them and roughly chop.

Meanwhile, in a medium saucepan, heat the olive oil over medium heat; add the garlic and cook until lightly browned, stirring constantly, about 2 minutes. Add the onion and cook until softened and translucent, about another 3 minutes. Add the tomatoes and oregano and season lightly with salt and pepper. Crumble the bouillon cube into the mixture and cook for about 2 minutes, until the ingredients start to blend.

Add the beef and mix well, breaking it up to avoid big lumps; cook until cooked through, 5 to 8 minutes. Season with salt, pepper, and nutmeg (but don't forget about the coming saltiness of the olives). Add ½ cup water, partially cover the pan, and reduce the heat to low. Cook until the ground meat is rich with flavor, about 25 minutes (you might add another tablespoon or so of water if needed). This can be done up to 3 days ahead of time.

Just before serving, fold in the chopped eggs, olives, and parsley.

Arroz de Forno
BAKED RICE WITH CHICKEN AND CHORIZO

Arroz de forno is a classic dish in any carioca's kitchen—there is always rice ready in the refrigerator, and we find many different recipes in which to use it. In Rio most cooks prepare this dish with precooked rice, but I prefer to use uncooked rice, for two reasons: First, it's less time-consuming; second, the aroma of cooked rice is fresher and the grain is even more fluffy, fragrant, and moist. This dish is extremely flexible, and you can opt to use other kinds of meat or vegetables. Follow the proportion of rice to stock to meat and you're off to a great meal!

SERVES 4

3 tablespoons extra virgin olive oil

1 chorizo (4 ounces), cut into ¼-inch slices

1 chicken breast (4 ounces), cut into ½-inch cubes

Kosher salt and freshly ground black pepper

½ small onion, finely chopped

2 scallions, white and green parts, chopped

3 garlic cloves, finely minced

2 plum tomatoes, peeled, seeded, and diced

1 cup white basmati or jasmine rice

3 cups chicken stock

4 ounces green beans, cooked and diced

Preheat the oven to 350°F and lightly coat a 7 x 11-inch baking dish with cooking spray.

Heat 1 tablespoon of the olive oil in a medium pot and add the chorizo; cook until lightly browned on both sides, about 2 minutes per side. Transfer the chorizo to the prepared baking dish, cover with aluminum foil, and set aside.

Season the chicken with salt and pepper. Add the remaining 2 tablespoons olive oil to the pot, add the chicken, and cook, stirring occasionally, for about 4 minutes, until just cooked through. Transfer to the same baking dish, spreading evenly over the chorizo, and cover with foil again.

Still using the same pot and any remaining oil left on the bottom (add a little more if necessary), add the onion and scallions, scraping the browned bits from the bottom of the pan. Add the garlic and cook for another minute. Add the tomatoes and cook, stirring with a wooden spoon, until the vegetables are softened, about 2 minutes.

Add the rice and stir quickly to coat well. Add the stock and bring to a boil. Season with salt and pepper. Uncover the chicken and chorizo. Carefully ladle everything from the pot into the baking dish. Mix in the green beans and slowly stir with a wooden spoon, distributing the ingredients evenly into the rice. Bake, uncovered, until the rice is cooked, about 25 minutes.

Remove from the oven and serve immediately.

Filé de Frango Enrolado no Minas Temperado
ROLLED CHICKEN BREAST WITH MINAS CHEESE AND FRESH HERBS IN MARIANA SAUCE

Chicken and Catupiry cheese are paired all over Rio (and all inside this book too!). Chicken and Minas cheese, on the other hand, not too often. Yet Minas cheese provides a lovely texture within the rolled chicken in this recipe. There is some work and technique involved, especially when it comes to butterflying and tying the meat. I must confess I have never mastered the butcher's way of using twine, and the two ends of the chicken breast always suffer from my poor tying skills. Even though I don't make the most perfect embroidery, once cooked and simmered in tomato sauce, the chicken looks gorgeous and always tastes sublime. If you can't find Minas cheese, you can use feta or ricotta salata instead.

SERVES 2–4

¼ cup chopped fresh parsley

¼ cup chopped fresh cilantro

1 tablespoon chopped fresh thyme

¼ cup freshly grated Parmesan cheese

⅓ cup grated or crumbled Minas cheese

1 garlic clove, minced

6 tablespoons extra virgin olive oil

Kosher salt and freshly ground black pepper

2 boneless, skinless chicken breasts (1½ pounds)

½ cup breadcrumbs

2½ cups prepared marinara sauce

In a medium bowl, combine the parsley, cilantro, thyme, Parmesan and Minas cheeses, garlic, and 4 tablespoons of the olive oil. Season with salt and pepper and mix with a rubber spatula.

On a cutting board, butterfly each chicken breast vertically. Place between a sheet of plastic wrap and pound thin and evenly, trying not to let it tear. Season with salt and pepper on both sides. Divide the filling among the chicken breasts and spread across the entire open surface. Roll up the chicken and tie with kitchen twine (alternatively, you can secure it with skewers).

Pour the breadcrumbs on a plate and roll the chicken breasts through them to coat lightly.

In a medium skillet, heat the remaining 2 tablespoons olive oil over medium heat. Add the chicken breasts and cook, turning, until lightly browned all over, 6 to 8 minutes.

Add the marinara sauce to the pan and bring to a simmer, scraping up the browned bits from the bottom of the pan with a wooden spoon. Simmer, turning occasionally, until the breasts are tender but firm.

Untie the chicken and cut into ¼-inch slices. Arrange on a plate and serve with the marinara sauce on the side.

Carne Assada de Panela com Batatas Douradas
BRAZILIAN-STYLE POT ROAST

I learned how to make this recipe from a friend's mother, Dona Angelina Aparecida Masieiro Braz, who is an awesome cook. It's healthy comfort food, a classic meat and potato dish. Dona Angelina uses water to cook the roast in, relying on the browning of the meat to give the sauce its full flavor and gorgeous mahogany color. I couldn't escape my formal culinary background, so I made the recipe with stock, resulting in a richer sauce. Chicken stock is what I have most frequently in my kitchen, so that's what I usually use, but any flavorful stock will work. (When I have leftover veal or beef bones, I don't let them go to waste and save them for stock—call me a stock maniac!). The potatoes become golden brown and tender as they cook in the sauce. You can also use brisket instead of beef chuck in this recipe. It is important to keep the pressure cooker at low heat at all times. If you don't have a pressure cooker, you can use a large pot or Dutch oven; add 1½ to 2 hours cooking time.

SERVES 4-6

3 pounds prime beef chuck

6 garlic cloves, grated

Kosher salt and freshly ground black pepper

2 tablespoons extra virgin olive oil

3 tablespoons vegetable oil

6 garlic cloves, sliced

1 quart chicken, beef, or veal stock or water

1½ pounds small Yukon gold potatoes, peeled

SPECIAL EQUIPMENT: pressure cooker

Rub the meat with the grated garlic, season with salt and pepper, and drizzle with the olive oil. Place the meat in a bowl, cover with plastic wrap, and refrigerate for at least 4 hours or preferably overnight. Bring the meat to room temperature 30 minutes before cooking.

Heat the vegetable oil in a pressure cooker over medium heat. Add the beef and sear, turning frequently, until lightly browned on all sides, 8 to 10 minutes.

Reduce the heat to low, scatter the sliced garlic around the meat, and cook until it is just golden brown, scraping the bottom of the pan occasionally. Don't go away; the garlic can turn from light golden to bitter dark very fast. Add the chicken stock, cover the pressure cooker, lock the lid, and cook at low pressure for about 1½ hours, checking every 30 minutes and turning the meat. Each time you check, make sure to let the pressure down from the pan first.

When the meat is done (it will shrink by almost one third), transfer to a bowl and immediately cover with aluminum foil. You should have a very dark sauce and the garlic will have seemed to disappear as it mingles with the juices.

Spread the potatoes evenly across the pan and cover them halfway with sauce. Cook the potatoes over low heat, with the pan uncovered at all times, turning occasionally to brown them evenly, about 12 minutes.

Return the meat to the pan with any accumulated juices, reheat to warm through, and serve.

Mousse de Chocolate Branca com Gelatina de Maracujá

WHITE CHOCOLATE MOUSSE WITH PASSION FRUIT GELÉE

Silky, sweet, and tart, this recipe brings me back to when I was fifteen years old, when I first developed a white chocolate mousse. I started with an American recipe that I got from Anne Willan's *Look & Cook* series and tried to make it work in my Brazilian kitchen. My first few attempts were failures, but there my mania for experimentation was born. This recipe is luxurious, the white chocolate mousse interlaced with a floral passion fruit gelée. The delicate pastel colors are beautiful, and you are sure to dazzle your guests with this dessert.

SERVES 8

MOUSSE

2 ounces white chocolate, finely chopped

2 large eggs, separated

1¼ cups heavy cream

Pinch of salt

2 tablespoons sugar

PASSION FRUIT GELÉE

1 teaspoon powdered gelatin

4 tablespoons water

½ cup passion fruit pulp, thawed

3 tablespoons sugar

SPECIAL EQUIPMENT:
8 six-ounces wine glasses

Make the mousse: Place the white chocolate in a bowl and set aside.

Place the egg yolks in a medium bowl and whisk lightly.

In a medium saucepan, bring ¾ cup of the heavy cream to a boil over medium heat. Pour a little of the hot cream into the yolks and whisk well, then pour in the remaining cream and whisk again. Pour the mixture into the saucepan and cook over low heat until it coats the back of a spoon. Immediately strain the mixture through a fine sieve directly over the white chocolate and mix with a rubber spatula until well blended. Let cool to room temperature, 10 to 15 minutes.

In the bowl of an electric mixer fitted with the whisk attachment, whip the remaining ½ cup heavy cream at medium speed until soft peaks form. Set aside.

In another bowl of an electric mixer fitted with the whisk attachment, combine the egg whites with a pinch of salt and, starting at low speed, beat until they start foaming, then increase the speed until peaks form. Gradually add the sugar, turn the speed to medium-high, and beat until soft glossy peaks forms. Using a large spatula, fold the whipped cream into the white chocolate mixture, then gently fold in the egg whites.

Carefully divide the mousse among the wine glasses with a small ladle or a tablespoon. Fill each glass a little above halfway, leaving space for the gelée. Refrigerate for at least 4 hours, preferably overnight.

Make the gelée: In a small bowl, dissolve the gelatin in the water. Stir and let stand until softened, about 2 minutes.

In a small saucepan, heat the passion fruit and sugar over low heat, whisking often to dissolve the sugar. Add the gelatin mixture and whisk well. Do not let it boil, otherwise the gelée will taste like gelatin.

Strain through a fine sieve into a measuring cup. Let cool to room temperature, 15 to 20 minutes, then pour into the wine glasses over the mousse. (If you let it stand too long, the gelée will start to harden and it won't pour as well, but it shouldn't be too hot, or it will melt the white mousse.) Transfer the glasses to the refrigerator and chill until the gelée is set, at least 2 hours. Remove the wine glasses from the refrigerator about 20 minutes before serving.

Arroz Docea
BRAZILIAN RICE PUDDING

Growing up there was always a batch of rice pudding in the fridge. Rather than eating it for dessert, I'd always stop by the kitchen after school and nosh on a bowlful for a little something sweet. As you cook this pudding, the mixture will seem a little soupy, but the beauty of this recipe is that the pudding thickens to a perfect consistency after chilling overnight. In Rio we use common long-grain white rice, but I like to use Arborio rice, yielding a starchier and fatter grain of rice. You can also use basmati or jasmine rice.

SERVES 6–8

Two 3-inch cinnamon sticks

4 cups whole milk

½ cup Arborio rice

2 tablespoons sugar

One 14-ounce can sweetened condensed milk

2 large egg yolks

Ground cinnamon for garnish

Smack the cinnamon stick on a cutting board with the flat side of a chef's knife to break it up lightly.

In a large saucepan, combine 3 cups of the whole milk, the rice, sugar, and cinnamon sticks. Bring to a boil, then reduce the heat and simmer, uncovered, stirring occasionally with a wooden spoon and making the rice doesn't stick to the bottom, until the rice is cooked through, about 20 minutes. Remove from the heat.

In another saucepan, combine the sweetened condensed milk and the remaining 1 cup whole milk.

In a medium bowl, whisk the egg yolks. Pour a little of the condensed milk in to temper, whisk well, then return everything back to the saucepan. Cook over low heat, stirring slowly and constantly with a wooden spoon, until the mixture just begins to boil, about 5 minutes. Combine the mixtures from the two pans and cook, stirring constantly, without letting it come to a boil, another 5 minutes.

Transfer the rice pudding to a bowl. You'll be tempted to taste it now; if you do, the rice will seem slightly sweet and too loose. Cover and refrigerate for at least 6 hours, preferably overnight. The cinnamon stick will continue to flavor the pudding, so remove it only just before serving.

Pour the pudding into a serving bowl or divide it among individual bowls, lightly sprinkle ground cinnamon on top, and serve cold.

Bolo da Benza
BENZA'S ALMOND CAKE

Although my name—Leticia—might be difficult to pronounce in English, Leticia is a very popular name in Portuguese (as well as in Spanish, French, and Italian). In my high school there were several Leticias, and in my classroom alone there were three of us. To make things easier, our classmates decided to nickname us all by our last name (although between us Leticias we called ourselves Lê). My maiden name is Leticia Moreinos Benzaquen, and so, around the sweet age of twelve, I became Benza. To this day, I have friends in Rio to whom I will always be Benza.

I love reuniting with friends in Rio and cooking dinner for them. Not too long ago, I invited some girlfriends over and served this almond cake, a version of a recipe I got from my dear friend and food writer David Leite. I remember the day David and I cooked together and photographed this cake for his website, leitesculinaria.com. I couldn't stop raving about it. Back in Rio, my friends went crazy over my adaptation of this almond cake, which they baptized as *Bolo da Benza* (Benza's Cake). Every now and then I receive an e-mail when someone makes the cake. It always comes with a little "miss you and our dinners together," which brings me joy, tears, and hunger to try new recipes with them the next time I am in Rio. Hopefully soon, my friends.

SERVES 6–8

3 cups blanched slivered almonds (see Tip)

1¼ cups sugar

12 tablespoons unsalted butter

4 large eggs, separated

½ teaspoon ground cinnamon

½ teaspoon vanilla extract

½ teaspoon almond extract

⅛ teaspoon salt

COOKING TIP: Don't use almond flour instead of slivered almonds. It's very easy to turn the nut mixture into paste and it might bring the cake down.

Center a rack in the middle of the oven and preheat the oven to 350°F. Grease a 10-inch springform pan with cooking spray, line the bottom with parchment paper, spray the parchment, and dust with flour.

In the bowl of a food processor, place the almonds and ¼ cup of the sugar, and beat until just ground (be careful not to overbeat—you don't want to release any oil from the nuts). Add the butter and pulse just until well incorporated (again, don't over mix).

In the bowl of an electric mixer fitted with the paddle attachment, beat the egg yolks and ½ cup of the sugar until pale and thick, 6 to 8 minutes. Add the cinnamon, vanilla, and almond extract and beat.

In another clean bowl of an electric mixer fitted with the whisk attachment, whip the egg whites with the salt. When they start to rise, slowly add the remaining ½ cup sugar and beat until soft peaks form.

Add one third of the egg whites and incorporate into the batter, then add the remaining whites, making sure the batter remains light and fluffy.

Pour the batter into the prepared pan and smooth the top with an offset spatula. Bake the cake until golden brown and the sides pull away from the pan, 40 to 45 minutes. The center will collapse a little, and that's normal. Transfer to a wire rack and let rest for 10 minutes before unmolding, then cool completely before serving.

GLOSSARY

Botequim

A *botequim* carries a lot of meaning for a carioca. Also called *boteco* or *bar*, the word comes from the Portuguese *botica* and from the Spanish *bodega*, referring to a place where food and drink are sold. In Rio (and in all of Brazil), the word *botequim* came to be a type of restaurant where people gather to drink and talk without much sense of time, after work or after the beach, with a certain party feeling. Recently *botequims* have been joined by more upscale cousins, a little newer and a littler cleaner, so cariocas created slang words; *pé-sujo* and *pé-limpo* ("dirty feet" and "clean feet") as a way to distinguish between the types of *botequims*.

Carioca

A person born in Rio de Janeiro. The word comes from the Native Indian *tupi* and translates to "white men."

Cachaça

Cachaça is a distilled beverage from Brazil, as important to the country as vodka is to Russia and tequila is to Mexico. Essentially, it is an *aguardente*: a spirit distilled from fruits or vegetables, in this case, the juices of the sugar cane. Cachaça is distinct from rum, though, which is made from molasses, not cane juice.

Catupiry cheese

Catupiry is a Brazilian cream cheese made from fresh cow's milk, yeast, heavy cream, sour cream, and salt. It was first developed in 1911 by Mario Silvestrini, an immigrant from Ravenna, Italy, who opened a tiny little store in Minas Gerais with his sister, Isaira. Since 1949, however, the cheese has been manufactured in Bebedouro, in the region of São Paulo. Burnished gold in color, catupiry has a dense, creamy texture, is slightly sweet and remains a key ingredient in classic Brazilian dishes. There are other types of cream cheese in Brazil, though we refer to them as *requeijão*, which has a thinner consistency. The name *catupiry* comes from the Native Indian *tupi-guarani* language; it means "excellent."

Azeite de dendê (dendê oil)

This oil is the mainstay of Bahian cuisine, and is the product extracted from the dendê palm tree, which was brought to Brazil by African slaves, back in the seventeenth century. The dendê palm tree is one of the most oleaginous in the world, producing more oil than soybeans, peanuts or coconut. The fruit and the pit are used in two different ways. The dendê oil used in cooking is extracted from the fruit pulp; first it is cooked in steam, then it is dried completely in the sun. The fruit is then crushed to release its bright orange-red oil. The pit is also used to extract oil of a different kind, with a transparent color, mostly used for cosmetics for its similarity to cocoa butter. Often sediment forms on the bottom of a dendê oil bottle. To liquefy, simply place the bottle in a bowl with warm water and let it sit for 20 minutes.

Doce de leite (dulce de leche)

This is truly a Latin ingredient produced and used all over South America. In Brazil, the state of Minas Gerais is dairy country and the biggest producer of the best dulce de leche. Essentially, dulce de leche is milk and sugar cooked slowly until it reaches the consistency of a caramelized paste. In Brazil we eat dulce de leche in all kinds of consistencies: as a candy, as a soft paste, hard paste, more sweet, less sweet, even diet. For all of the recipes in this book, I used canned Nestlé dulce de leche.

Carne seca (jerk meat)

Carne seca is a huge part of Brazilian cooking. In Portuguese we also call it *carne de sol*, referring to salt-cured and sun-dried meat. Most jerk meats come from a lean cut, such as beef silverside, because too much marbled fat (which gives that buttery richness we want in our cooked meats) makes the dried meat too tough. Most pieces of jerk meat are cut against the grain to make them tender rather than leathery. The processes of making American jerk beef vary greatly, from salting to brining, smoking in hickory or oak, or not smoking at all. Flavoring can be introduced with a dry rub, a paste, or a marinade. Drying can take place in commercial ovens, dehydrators, or naturally. The Brazilian method is less elaborate. While many of the ingredients found in this country are comparable to those found in Brazil, jerk meat is the exception, so it might taste a little different from the one eaten in Brazil. Most Brazilian stores in the US carry a ready-made version of prepared *carne seca* that I use in some of the recipes in this book.

Linguiça

Linguiça is a type of sausage from Portugal that was brought to Brazil during colonial times. Today *linguiça* is the most adored sausage in Brazil, served in *churrascarias* (our barbecue restaurants) as hors d'oeuvres and in dishes such as *feijoada*, *farofa*, soups, and grills. The robust sausage is made from cured pork meat and flavored with onion, garlic, and seasonings. When cooking *linguiça*, never poke the link; you don't want any fat to escape, as this is what makes the *linguiça* so moist and tender. If you can't find it, you can use chorizo or fresh sausage instead.

Manioc (tapioca) starch

Manioc starch (*povilho doce*) and sour manioc starch (*povilho azedo*) are both extracted from yucca (aka manioc or cassava). To obtain the starch, the vegetable is finely grated, mixed with water, and strained over a thick layer of cheesecloth or a fine sieve. The wet pulp is left to rest in a bucket for a day to allow the starch to sink to the bottom and completely separate from the water which, by that time, has turned yellow. To make the sour manioc starch (*povilho azedo*), this first step is prolonged for at least 15 days, until the starch is fermented under water.

This yellow water is then discarded and the process is repeated—the starch accumulated at the bottom of the bucket is scraped, mixed again with new water, sieved again through the cheesecloth, and placed in a bucket to sit for another day.

This time around, the water will be clearer and the starch accumulated on the bottom will be snow white. The water is again discarded, the starch is scraped and spread onto flat sheet pans to dry. Finally, the starch is sieved to ensure a very fine consistency.

When it comes to manioc and tapioca starch, it can get very confusing because different American brands call these products different names. See below for some clarity.

Povilho doce (manioc starch or sweet manioc starch)

Goya calls it Tapioca Starch, but Bob's Red Mill calls it Tapioca Flour, and I call it manioc starch in this book.

Povilho azedo (sour or fermented manioc starch)

No American brand makes the Brazilian equivalent of sour manioc starch (at least not yet), so when a recipe calls for this ingredient, do not substitute for an American brand. I recommend Yoki or Gloriasul brands.

Farinha de mandioca (manioc flour)

Although this flour is also extracted from the yucca vegetable, the process is completely different from making starch. Here, the yucca vegetable is not washed but ground, then squeezed in a cloth to eliminate any vegetable juices, sieved, and lightly toasted. Think of it as breadcrumbs. *Farinha de mendioca* is used to make another important staple of Brazilian cuisine: farofa.

Minas cheese

Minas cheese is to Brazil what feta is to Greece, or what mozzarella is to Italy. The taste is also a cross between feta, ricotta, and mozzarella. Brazilians eat Minas cheese throughout the country, but Mineiros (people born in Minas Gerais) are really proud to have created it in their state of Minas Gerais, hence the name. Minas cheese, made from cow's milk, is white, fresh, and firm. Like other fresh white cheeses, Minas has a way of complementing other flavors without masking them, and it definitely deserves more attention on its own. It is mostly consumed fresh, but the cheese can also be ripened to various degrees: *fresco* (fresh), *meia-cura* (semi-ripened), and *curado* (ripened).

Bacalhau salgado (salt cod)

Salt cod arrived on the Brazilian table through our colonizers, and today Brazil is the biggest consumer of salt cod followed by Portugal, Spain, and Italy. Brazil, however, is not a producer—all salt cod is imported from Norway and Portugal. Brazilians rarely eat fresh cod as it's just not available to us. Once reconstituted, salt cod presents a flaky flesh that is absolutely delicious. The best species of cod for salting is the Atlantic cod, *Gadus morhua*. When using salt cod, it's very important to de-salt it properly: Use a big plastic container as the volume of water has to be at least 10 times bigger than the weight of the cod. I also like to use a rack or colander so the cod is floating completely in the water. Try to find salt cod that has thick flesh.

Yucca

This tuber vegetable also goes by the names *manioc* or *cassava*. Earthier tasting than a potato and richer in starch, this vegetable is one of the foundations of Brazilian cooking. It comes from a perennial shrub with origins in the Amazon. The plant's long roots grow in clusters and are covered in a thick, shiny brown skin, and a thick white layer. When cut off, the outer layers reveal a snow white, firm interior with grey or purple veins. The center of the vegetable also carries a woody fiber that is not pleasant to eat, but is easy to remove. Riper yuccas usually contain less fibre in their centers. Generally speaking, the thicker the yucca, the riper it is. There are so many derivatives of this one vegetable: toasted flour, flakes, starches, juices. Even the skin and leaves are used in some parts of Brazil. For home use, yucca is mostly boiled or fried and becomes very creamy with a mellow taste. When buying yucca, try to look for an even-colored vegetable with slightly waxy brown skin and no soft or moldy spots. Many of the yuccas sold in the United States are coated with a thin layer of wax to help extend shelf life.

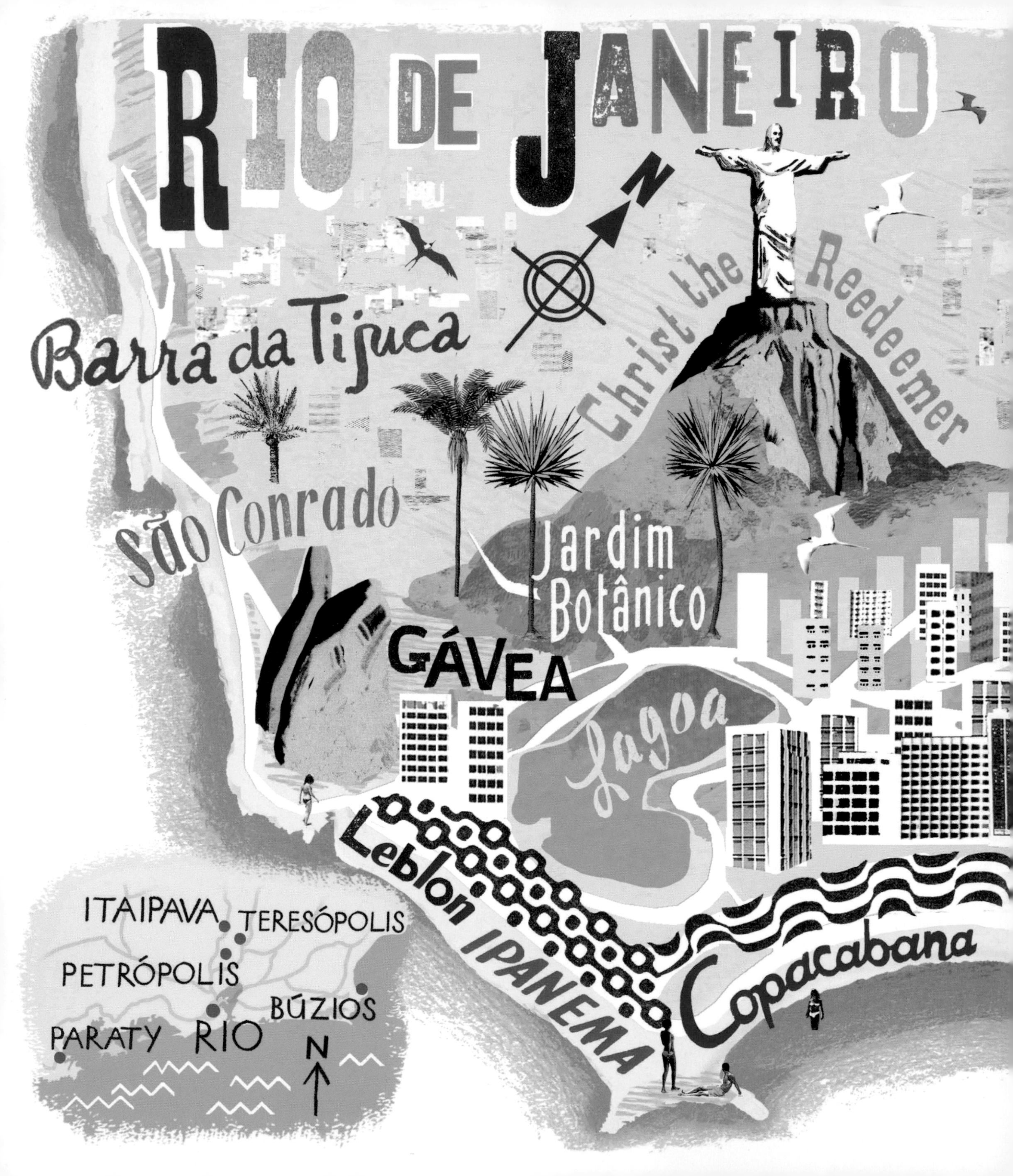

RIO DE JANEIRO

Barra da Tijuca

São Conrado

Christ the Reedeemer

N

Jardim Botânico

GÁVEA

Lagoa

Leblon IPANEMA

Copacabana

ITAIPAVA TERESÓPOLIS

PETRÓPOLIS

PARATY   RIO   BÚZIOS

N

Ponte Rio Niteroi

NITEROI

CENTRO

LAPA

SANTA TERESA

Laranjeiras

GLÓRIA

COSME VELHO

FLAMENGO

Botafago

SUGAR LOAF MOUNTAIN →

LEME

INDEX

ACKNOWLEDGMENTS

This book is really special to me, not only because it's a tribute to my hometown of Rio de Janeiro, but also because it kept me in two places at once: Rio and Connecticut. I am equally grateful to both, where most of my life takes place.

I grew up and became obsessed with food in Rio, but it was in Connecticut that I built my personal and professional life, thanks to the people who believed in my work.

It all started with Joy Tutela—and I am forever grateful for your guidance and continuous support. I am also grateful for the team at Westport Entertainment, Bill Stankey, Tyler Delaney, and Mary Lalli for believing in my dreams and my work.

This is my second book with Kyle Books and I can't thank them enough for that. Thank you, Anja Schmidt, for being a great editor; working with you makes me a better author. Thank you, Kate Sears, for the beautiful photos, Paul Grimes for making Rio's food look as beautiful as the city, and PJ Mehaffey for all the beautiful props. Thank you, Julie Grey and Sara Mae Danish, for testing my recipes.

No Rio de Janeiro, obrigada a todos aqueles que abriram suas portas para mim e diviram suas histórias, segredos, e receitas. Meus jantares são deliciosos por causa disso e sem vocês, este livro não seria o mesmo.

Bemdita foi a hora em que conheci o fotógrafo carioca Ricardo Mattos *em NY. É uma honra ter fotos suas da nossa cidade maravilhosa.*

Obrigada a todos os meus amigos no Rio, especialmente Tatiana El-Mann Cohen *que além de grande amiga, foi uma ótima guia organizando viagens divertidas com nossas crianaças.*

Obrigada ao meu analista José Alberto Zusman.

Obrigada ao meu irmão Jimmy Benzaquem*, sua esposa* Fernanda*, e meus sobrinhos, Nicolas e Valentina, por estarem sempre do meu lado.*

Obrigada aos meus pais por amenizar a dor de morar longe da familia, e por recortar artigos de jornais e revistas que serviram como inspiracao para esse livro. Essas palavras são poucas para agradecer todo o amor e tudo o que vocês fazem por mim e por minha familia.

Todos os esforcos foram realizados no sentido de obter as autorizacoes das pessoas retratadas nas fotos originais do arquivo pessoal da Autora. No entanto, apesar do evidente consentimento, não conseguimos localiza-las. Razão pela qual estão reservados os direitos de imagem para atender eventuais futuras reivindicaçoes.

Thank you to the Ribacks for being a loving family and for your constant support. Thank you to all of my friends for being part of my life and sharing many meals together. Thank you also to Patti Billone.

To my handsome husband Dean, thank you for sharing your life with me and for your infinite love.

Aos meus filhos, Thomas *e* Bianca, *vocês são o ar que respiro, o sol e a lua do meu céu.*

Obrigada a minha cidade maravilhosa, Rio de Janeiro, que continua muito lindo! É uma honra dedicar este livro a você!

And finally, I want to thank everyone who bought my first cookbook and stayed in touch over the years, sending pictures, comments, and always eager to cook more Brazilian food.